COZY WOOD INTERIORS

LINKS

COZY WOOD INTERIORS

Edition 2009

Work conception: Carles Broto

Graphic design and production: Roberto Bottura, architect

Texts: contributed by the architects

© Carles Broto i Comerma

Jonqueres, 10, 1-5, Barcelona 08003, España

Tel.: +34-93-301-21-99

Fax: +34-93-301-00-21

info@linksbooks.net

www.linksbooks.net

All rights reserved. No part of this book may be used or reprduced in any manner whatsoever without written permission except in the case of brief quotations embodied in critical articles and reviews.

COZY WOOD INTERIORS

LINKS

Index

008	oos ag open	154	Blauraum Architekten
	House-Sculpture		Studio Blauraum
018	Architeam 4	164	Hanrahan & Meyers
	Living Box		Loft Holley
028	Susan T. Rodríguez	176	Eva Prats y Ricardo Flores
	Island Cabin		A house in a suitcase
038	XTEN Architecture	186	JAHN Associates
	VHouse		Kutti Beach House
050	Dieter Thiel	198	Felipe Assadi
	Bangert Studio and House		Buzeta House
060	Daigo Ishii + Future-Scape	208	Peter Hulting Architect
	Cottage in Kawanishi		Guest Appearance
076	Smiths Architects	218	Drexler Guinand Jauslin
	Smith McLain Cabin		Weekend House
088	José Cruz Ovalle	230	EDGE DESIGN INSTITUTE
	House in Santo Domingo		Suitcase House
098	Taylor Smyth Architects	244	José Cruz Ovalle
	Sunset Cabin		Study and Home in Vitacura
108	Nendo	252	Jean-Pierre Lévêque
	Drawer-House		Maison Rue Compans
122	Pierre Thibault	264	Littow architectes
	Beaver's Lake Refuge		Paris 6e
134	Cesare Leonardi	276	Arnaud Goujon Architecte
	Casa Mescoli-Goich		Transformed penthouse
146	Fuhrimann & Hächler	290	Jarmund/Vigsnaes Architects
	Holiday house on the Rigi		Red House

Introduction

Despite being one of the oldest building materials, it is one that there need be no shortage of if wisely managed, as more will grow to replenish the supply. Wood is alive and a home built out of it ultimately becomes a paradigmatic connection between architecture and life. The architects and all interiors featured in this book have in common their fascination regarding the richness, the texture, and the strength of wood to enhance their creations. Though the spaces are small, space and light are maximized, superfluous elements are minimized, and the warm, sophisticated quality of wood glows throughout. Moreover, the sustainability of wood construction makes each item into a statement of environmental intentions. These works feature an astoundingly wide range of creative wood interiors. Each of the projects within this worldwide selection is clearly explained by the designers themselves and all of the examples selected share the highest degree of architectural quality due to innovative uses of wood as well as the architects outspoken bid for environmentally sustainable construction. Included in this volume are sophisticated residences, contemporary homes and apartments. Outstanding photographs accompany the working plans and clear text, to achieve an optimal communication of these buildings' main features, the materials used and their defining characteristics.

oos ag open operating system

House-Sculpture in an Alpine Environment

Feldis, Switzerland Photographs: Dominique Marc Wehrli

The main characteristics of the site for this holiday house were its steepness, its location 1,500 meters above sea level and the magnificent views to the surrounding valleys and mountains.

The architects' subtle approach created a timber building that follows the slope of the hill and is integrated into its environment.

Like a natural element, the building changes as the observer moves around it, appearing either slim and light or large and heavy, depending on the point of view. By opening or closing the large louver blinds, inhabitants of the house can also directly affect the external appearance of the house.

The layout of the house is simple, being divided into two zones. On one side are the individual rooms, with each room, including the kitchen and also the storage areas, conditioning the next. On the other side, an open space flows through the three levels from the entrance and through the cascading stairwell to the open-plan floor where the living room is located. This is a negative space, created by the shapes of the bedrooms and other private areas, which divides the house-sculpture into fluid and static zones. The slight rotation and displacement of the building allowed the architects to orient the rooms towards the spectacular alpine landscape.

Timber was chosen as the main construction material because it allowed for the greatest flexibility in relation to planning and structure, given the limitations of the location and building regulations. The fact that the brief was to design a simple holiday house to be used only during particular periods also allowed the architects to experiment with acoustic requirements. The reduced thickness of the internal construction elements simplified the project and created a larger living area.

The projecting roof in the terrace area took the construction system to its limits, emphasizing the sculptural quality of the building and the spatial variety that defines the house. The rough timber finish gives the desired feeling of a simple holiday house, which is carried through to the interiors in raw wood, and also expressed through the furnishings.

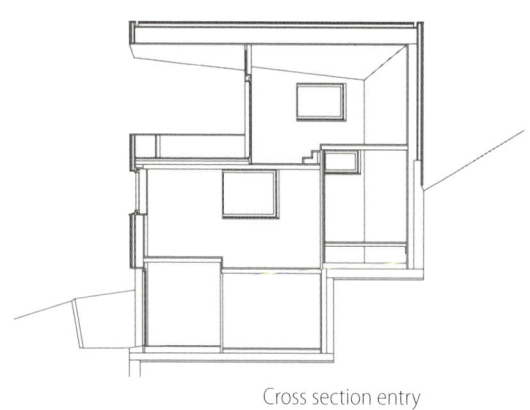

Cross section entry

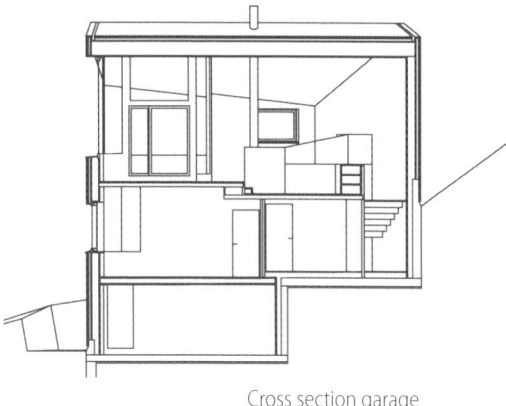

Cross section garage

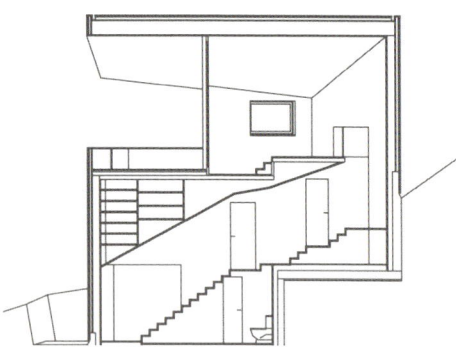

Cross section stair

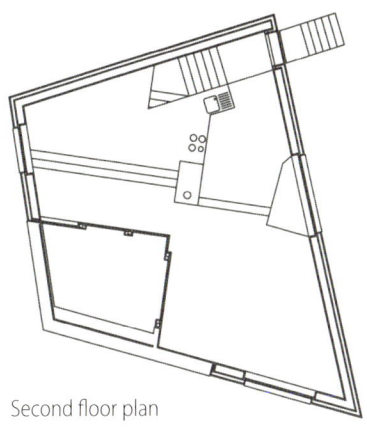

Second floor plan

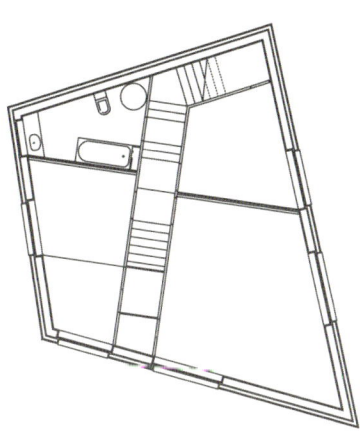

First floor plan

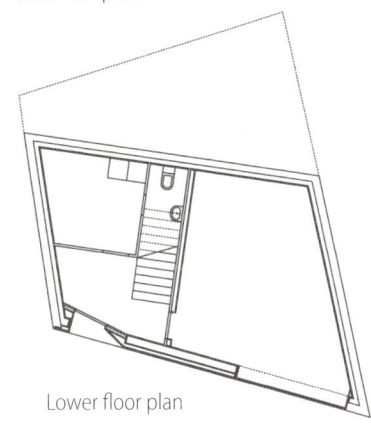

Lower floor plan

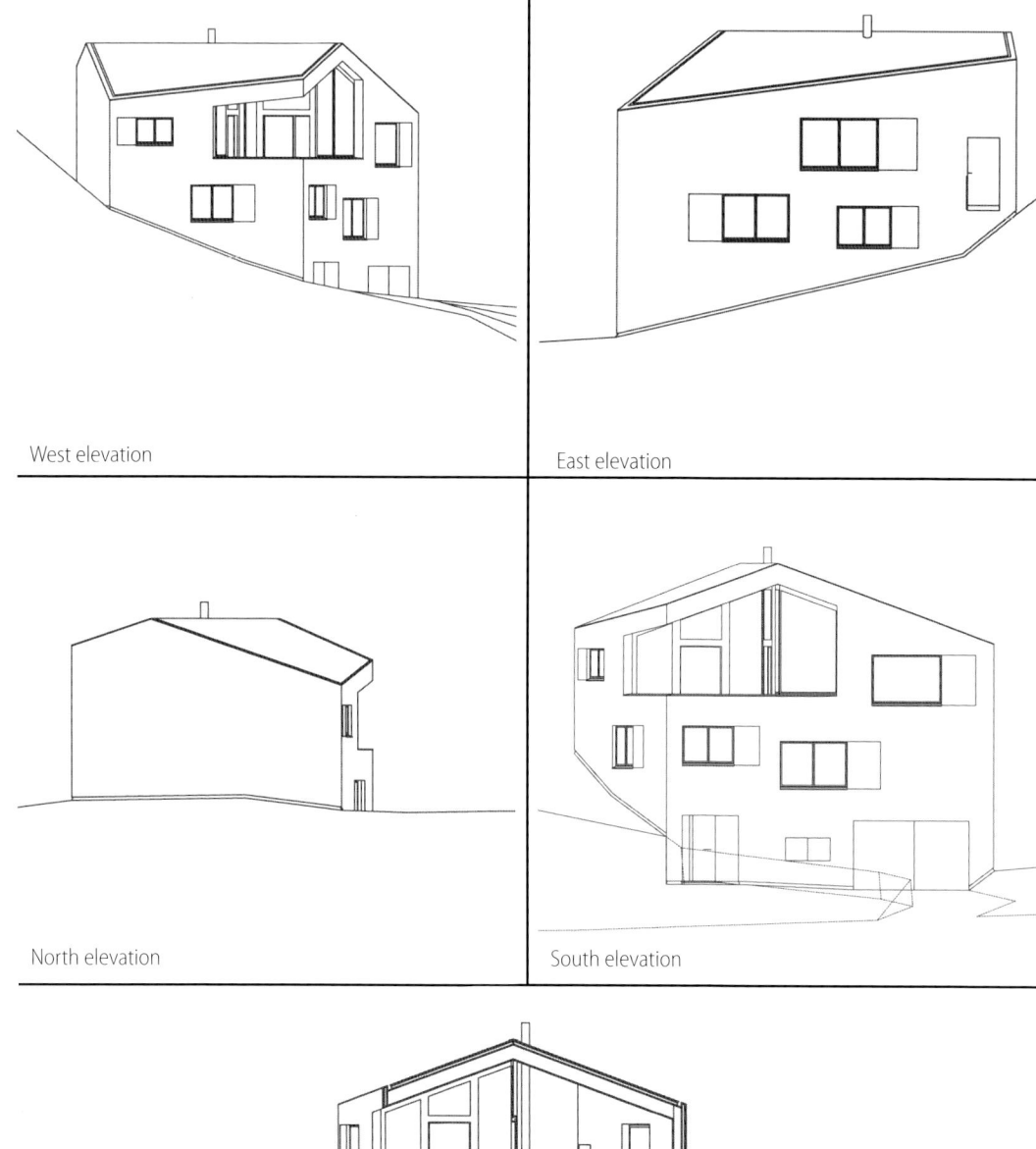

The building has been designed to be transformed by the passing of time. The larch timber facade and louvered windows will change as they age, as will the steel sheets that the architects have chosen to use instead of the usual concrete retaining walls. In this way the building will increasingly be integrated into the landscape.

Architeam 4

Living Box

KÜBLIS, SWITZERLAND *Photographs: Tom Kawara*

The house is located on a very steep site on the side of a hill, overlooking the town and with views out to the mountains. The architects decided early in the design process that the most solid option was to raise the building off the ground, meaning that only minimal foundation elements were required and leaving the grassy area under the house intact. From the invisible concrete foundations they erected an elegant steel structure to support the house, which was lined with spruce timber, except for the cube covered with Duripanel.

The house is approached via a steel bridge from a concrete platform that is used for parking.

It was designed to meet the needs of a modern family with three children, with special emphasis on optimum orientation and minimizing energy needs. On the side parallel to the hill, there is a line of bathrooms and services that run through the building and terminate in a series of balconies to the west. The floor containing the living room joins this line to the north, and covers the balconies on the west side. The roof terrace, located above the bedrooms and work areas, is accessed through the south-facing glazed area.

Part of the house construction is based on the cubic elements of the "Living Box" house designed by the same architects and carpenters, with building materials and construction methods that optimize solar energy. The inhabitants of a "Living Box" live in a kind of greenhouse optimized to their needs, and in spite of the scarce sunlight during the winter months, the house consumes eight times less than a conventional house. The insulated and hermetic skin of the building covers the volumes like a sweater, and the windows that break the surface are fitted with special glass and insulated. Sophisticated heating, ventilation, energy storage and domestic technology systems are integrated into the design of the house, making it extremely energy efficient, ideal for the owners and the environment.

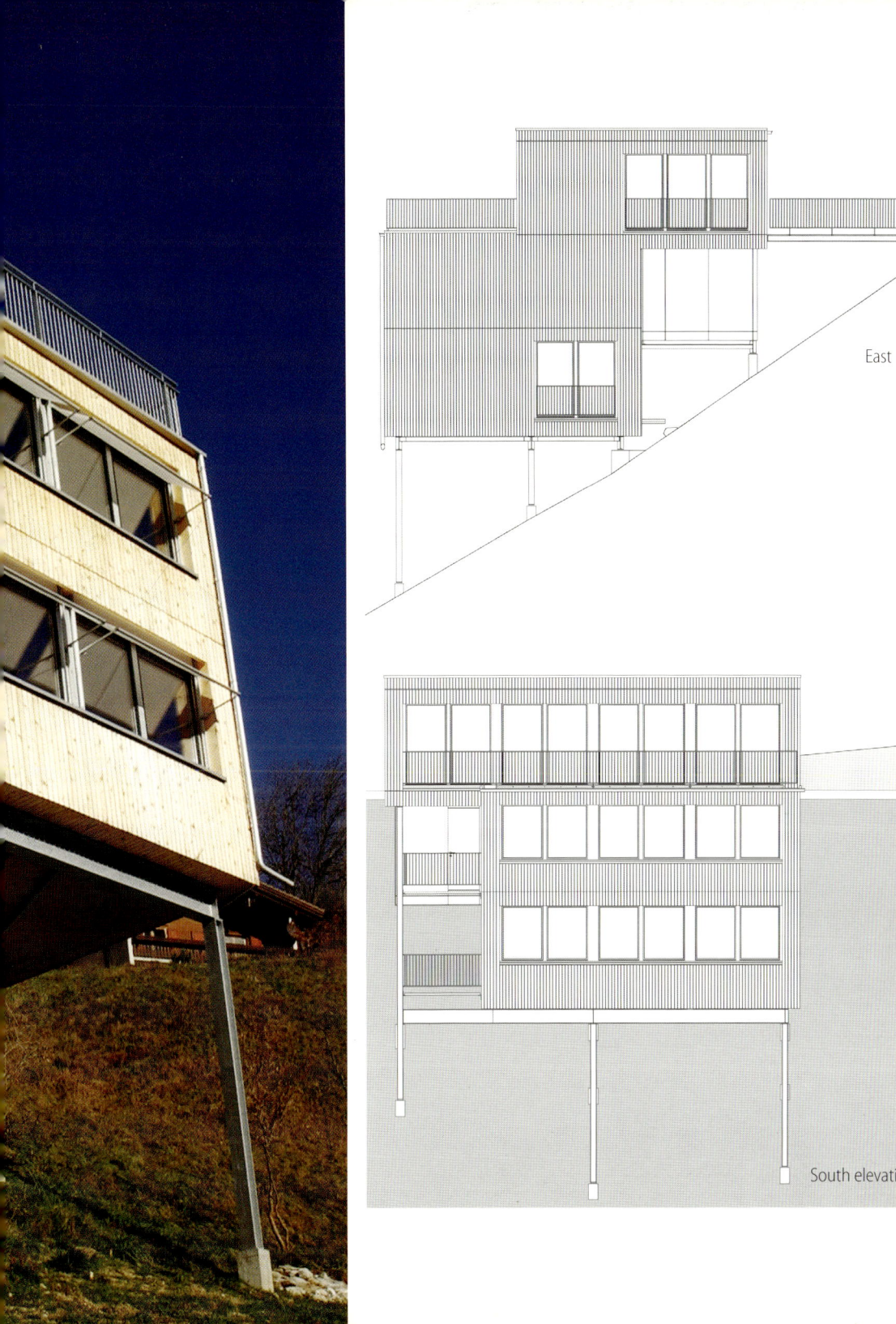

East Elevation

South elevation

The specially treated windows allow those in the house to enjoy the views and ample natural light, while conserving heat energy. The solar energy that enters the house through the windows is stored in the floors and ceilings, and reused through sophisticated recirculation systems.

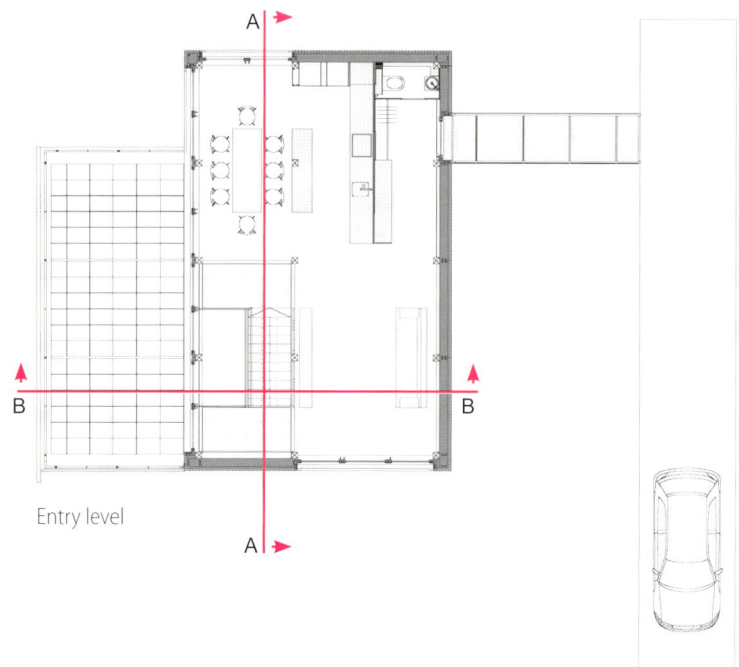

Entry level

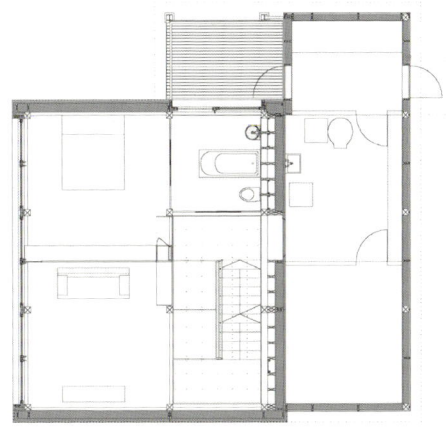
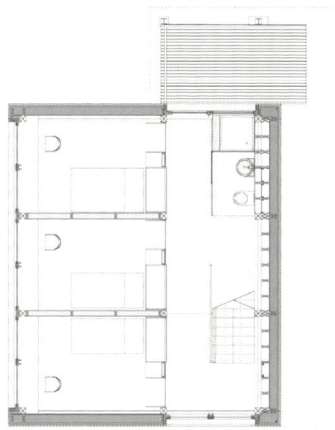

Level -1   Level -2

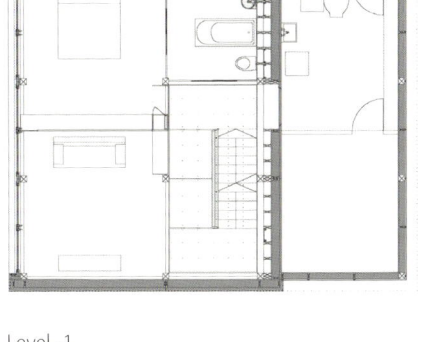

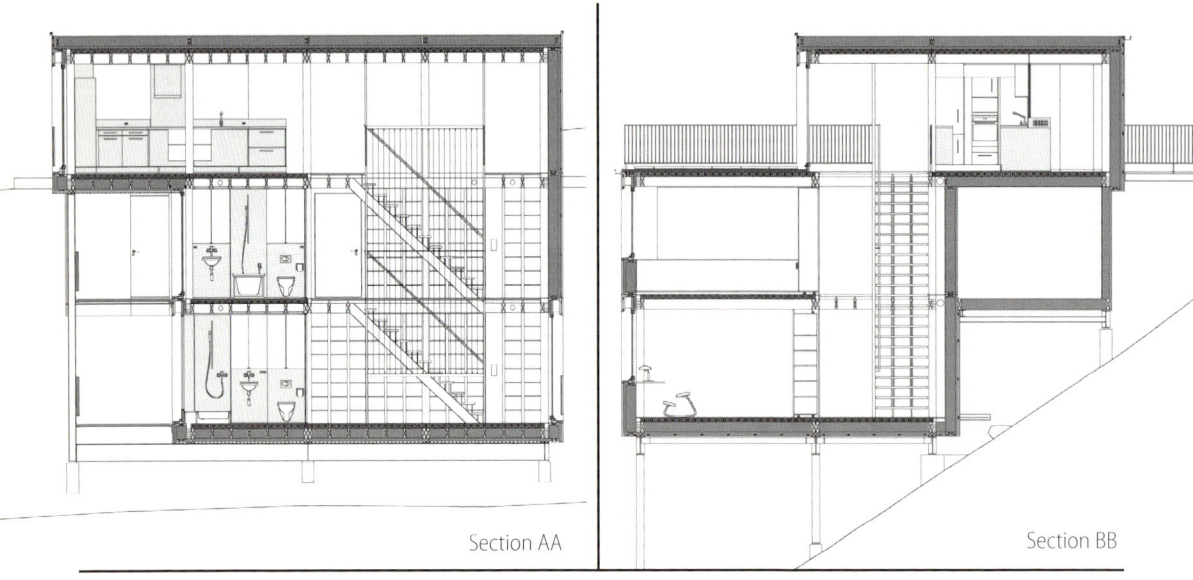

Section AA

Section BB

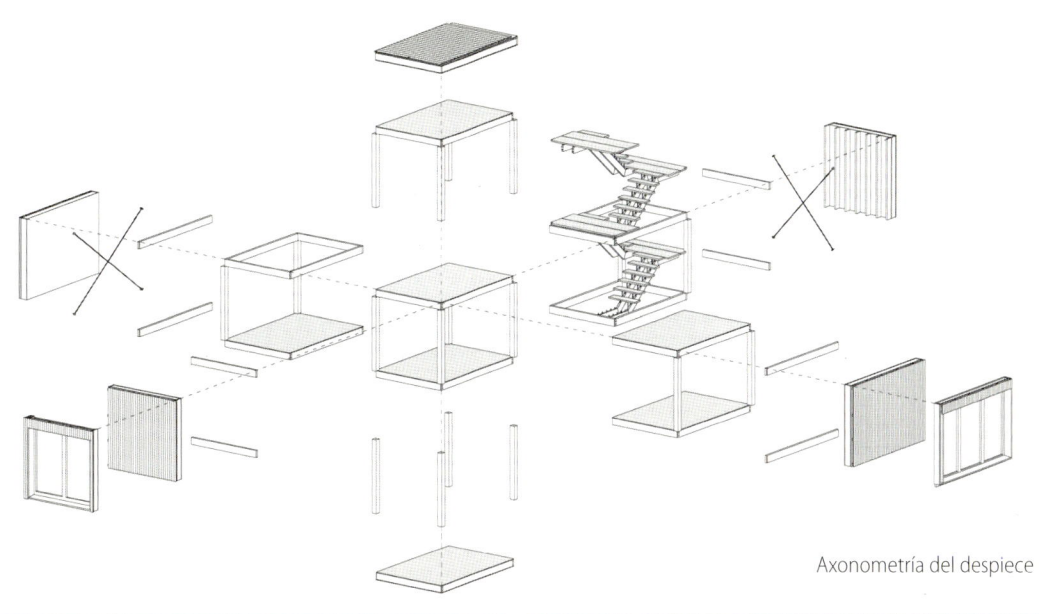

Axonometría del despiece

Susan T. Rodríguez

Island Cabin

PENOBSCOT BAY, MAINE, USA　　　　　　　　　　　　　　　　　*Photographs: Jeff Goldberg/Esto*

This seasonal cabin is located on a small private island in the Penobscot Bay approximately 12 miles off the coast of Maine. The cabin is situated on a bluff overlooking a narrow nautical passage. The overall building form is composed of two simple shed roof structures joined by a raised deck and walkway. These two pitched roof structures are essential to the water collection system for the island. The larger volume opens up to the water view and the smaller one to the wooded landscape from the water, yet still allows for dramatic views from within. The detail development of the cabin is intended to animate the simple structures with shade and shadow and highlight many of the functional aspects of the design; its gutter and downspout system, bracketed roof overhang, and shutters. The primary building material for the cabin is wood. A repetitive, pre-cut post and beam structure was erected on the site in two and a half days on a pressure-treated frame base. It is enclosed with laminated decking and cedar shingles. Cedar trim elements, wood windows, pine shutters and metal detailing complete the assembly. The shutters operate on sliding barn door hardware and galvanised hinges fabricate locally. A continuous clerestory window in the larger cabin disengages the sloping roof plane from the vertical wall surface, allowing the structure to visually penetrate from interior to exterior. The larger cabin is the main living space with sleeping accommodation on two levels and storage below. The smaller cabin provides flexible space for sleeping or recreation and houses three water cisterns below. The island has its own independent infrastructure. Propane powers the appliances and lighting, along with a small generator for pumping water and septic. A water tower, set at the island's highpoint, pressurises the system. A wood stove provides heat, when necessary during the season.

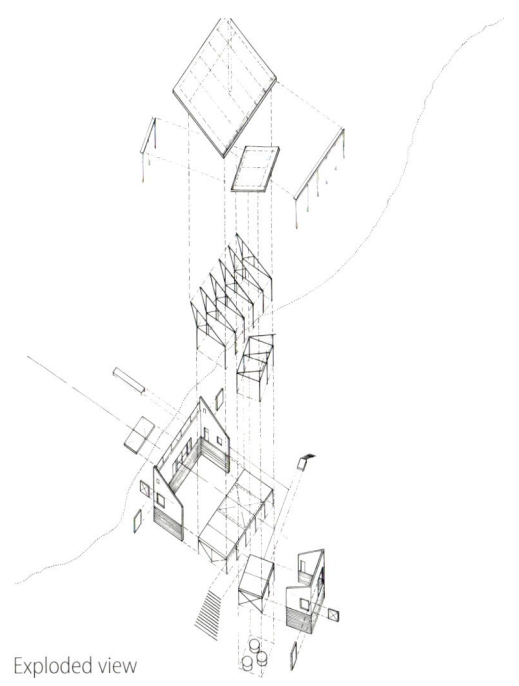

Exploded view

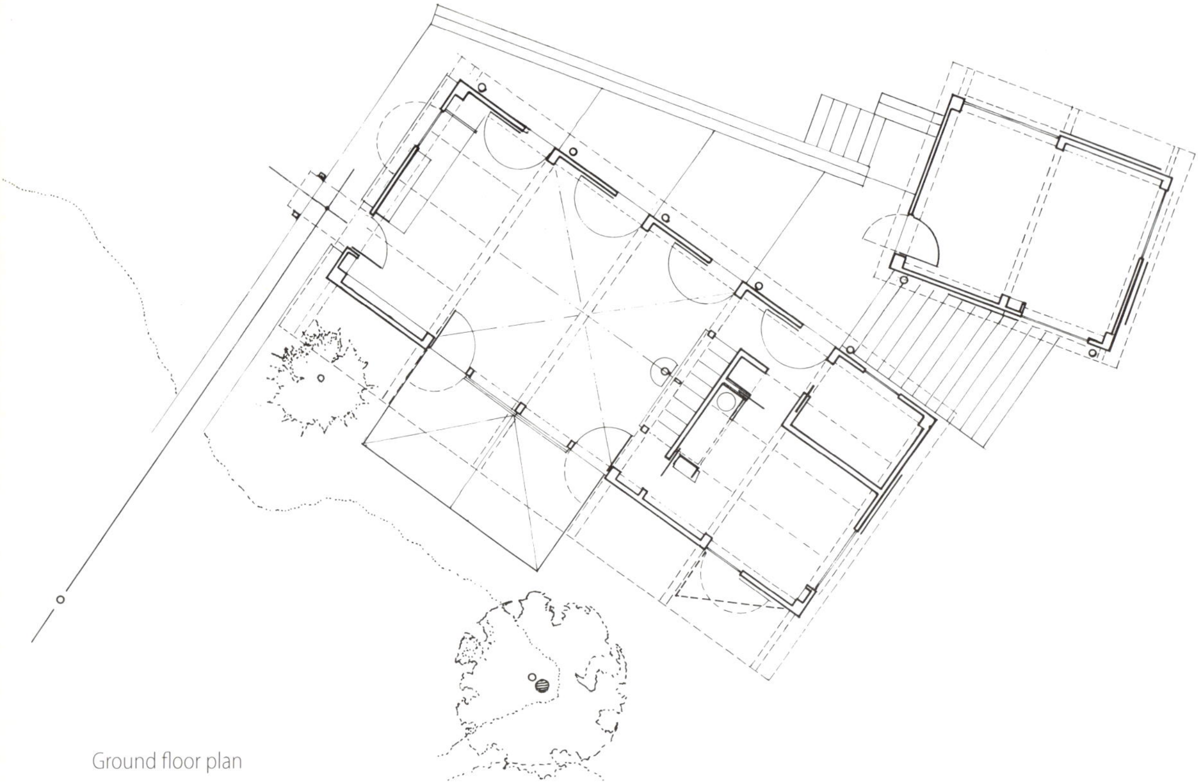

Ground floor plan

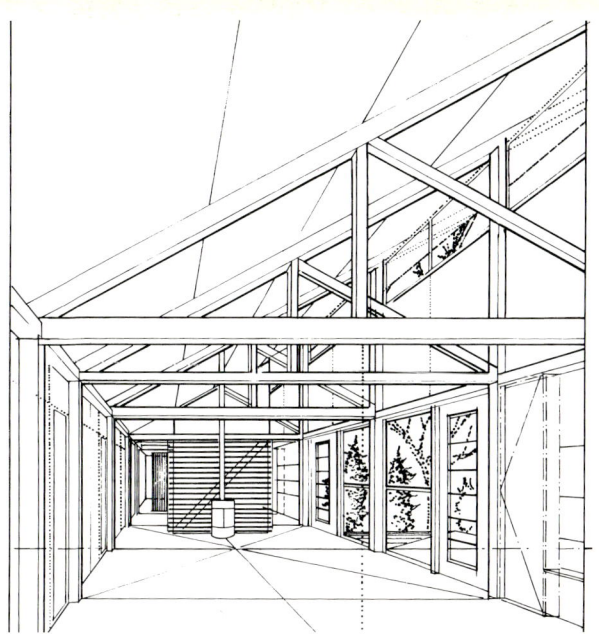

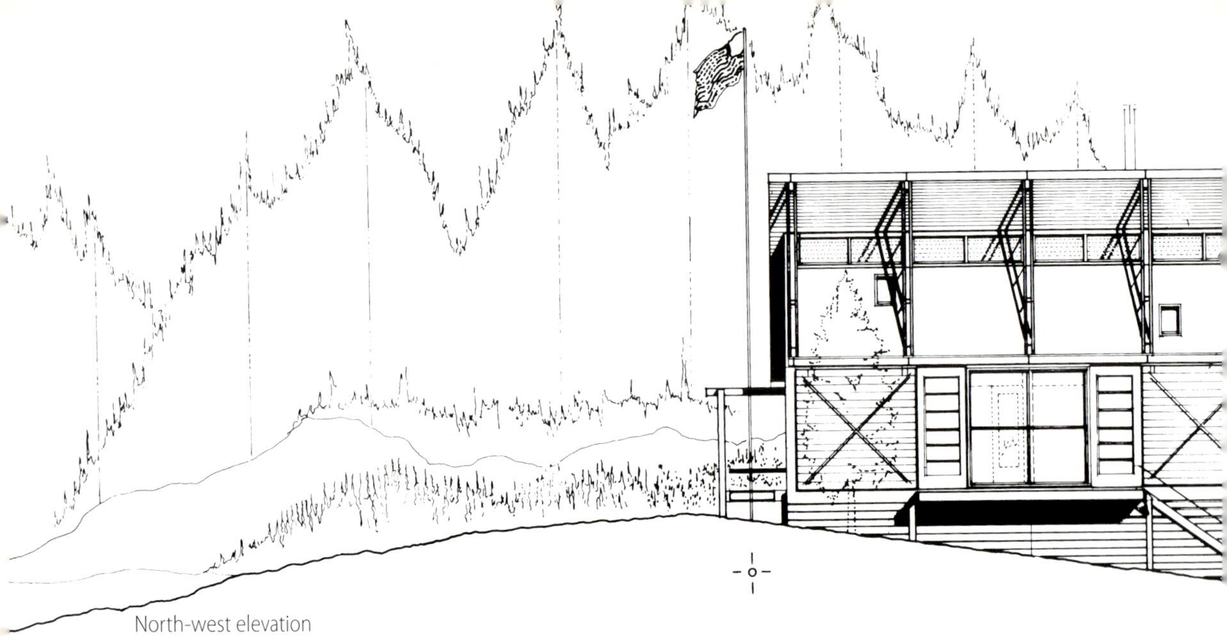

North-west elevation

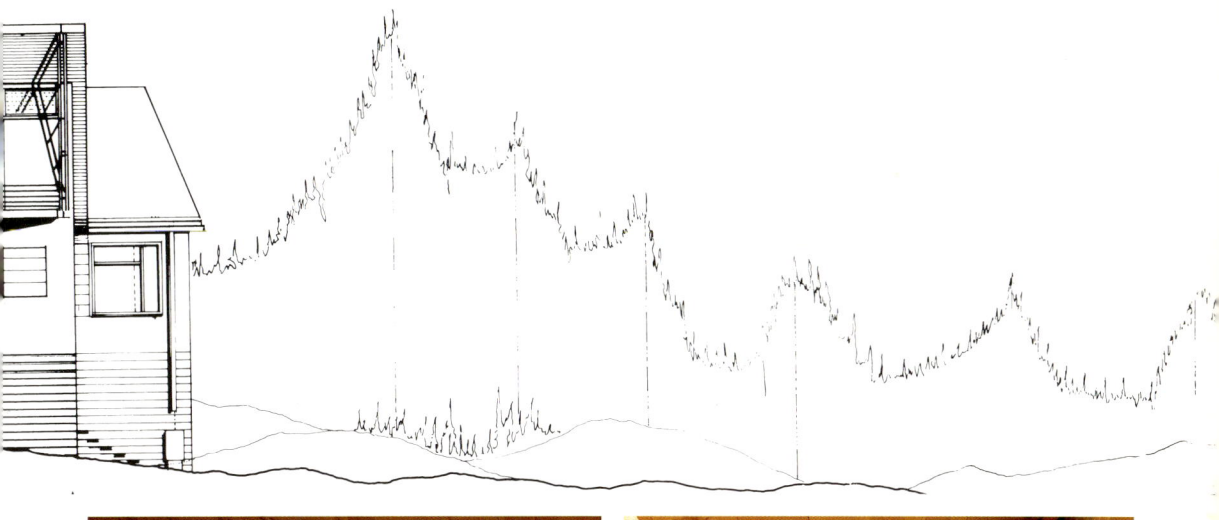

XTEN Architecture

Vhouse

Los Angeles, California, USA

Photographs: Art Gray

The Vhouse is located on a hillside street, set amongst tightly spaced small-scale stucco houses without any remarkable architectural qualities. The sloping canyon hillside to the rear of the site however, with its walnut and conifer trees, offered a wonderful environment for an open architecture linking inside and outside space.

Instead of a multistory volume that would dominate the setting, the architects chose a low courtyard installation that fits into the canyon plot like a pavilion. Four thick bearing walls are oriented perpendicular to the hillside and follow the site lines of the V-shaped lot. A series of laminated wood beams clear span between these walls and allow for large areas of the facade to open to the landscape. The folds and cantilevers of the roof geometry are articulated to respond to the specific conditions of the site.

The courtyard is planned as an outdoor room around which the different types of day and nighttime living are organized. Several sets of glass doors create a soft threshold between the living area and the courtyard. Direct access from the open kitchen allows for outdoor dining and entertaining throughout the year, while secondary openings in the bearing walls allow for access from the bedrooms in the mornings.

Inside, the four bearing walls define three distinct program zones. The central zone is planned as a single cohesive open space that offers, for the most part, a transparent indoor/ outdoor living space. Flanking this area are two wings that house the bedrooms and more private spaces of the program.

The detailing and materiality of the house is minimal yet indivisibly bound to its architectural concept. The thick bearing walls are clad in wide redwood planks that wrap continuously from exterior to interior and extend the landscape deep into the interior of the house through vertical glass panels. In contrast to these volumetric walls, the soft façades are treated as a surface texture of finely ribbed redwood slats spaced between floor to roof glass with fir framing. This framing is in turn connected to the spacing of the exposed roof structure, generating a series of continuous lines that articulate the interior space while also framing the exterior courtyard and canyon hillside beyond.

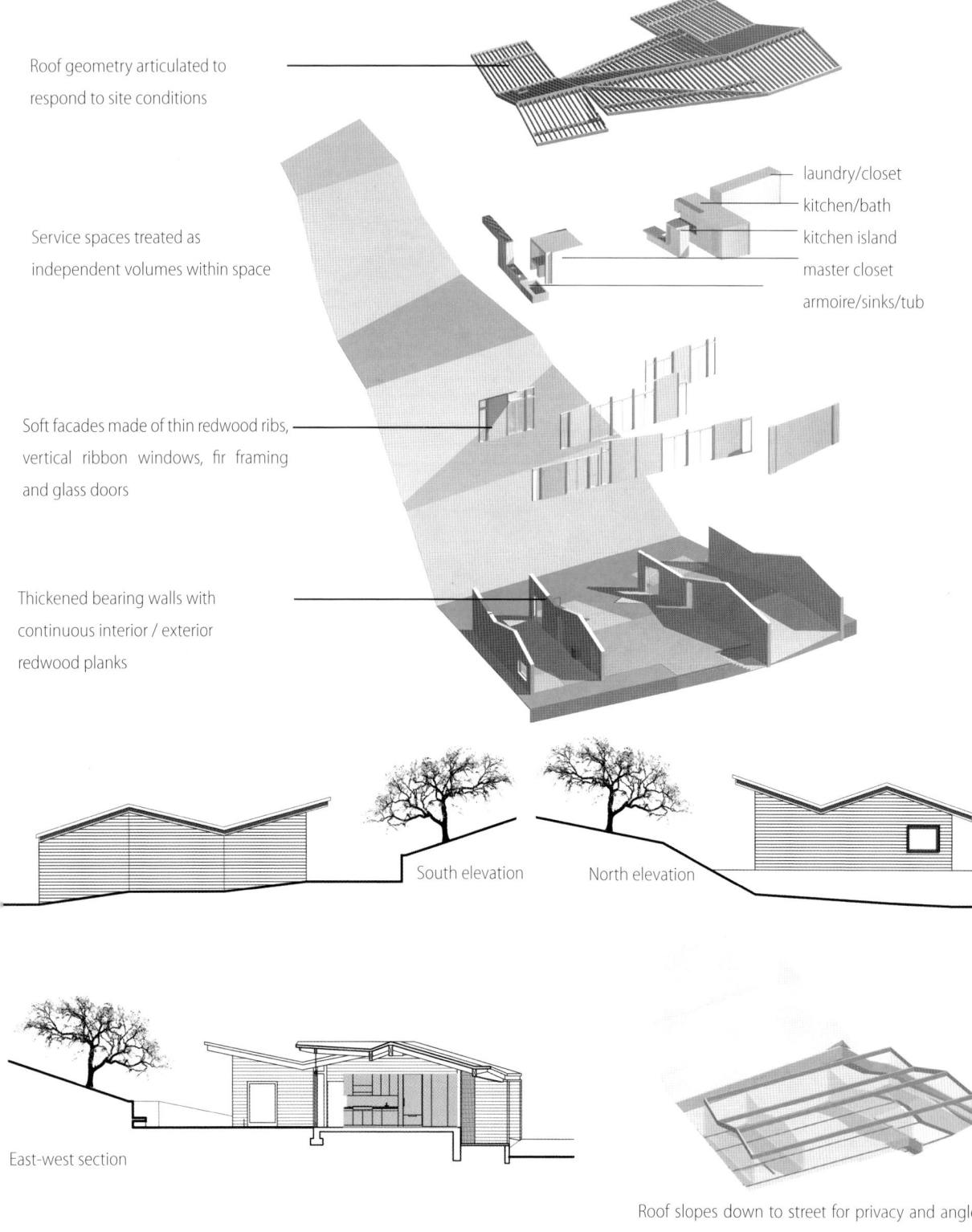

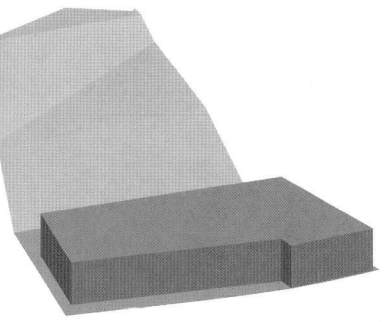

Maximum site coverage, given city setbacks

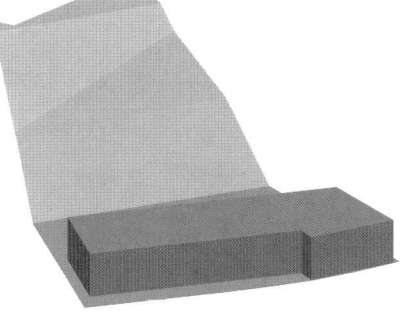

Concentration to street = larger garden area

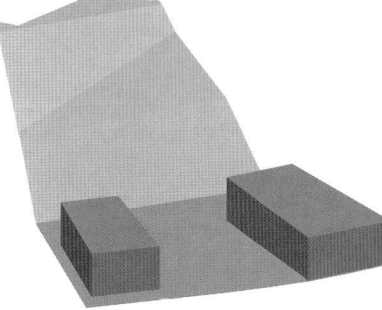

Two wings with courtyard = flow to landscape

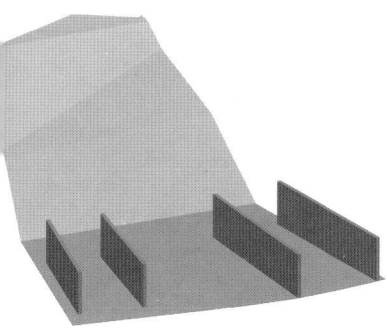

Four fin walls = three distinct program zones

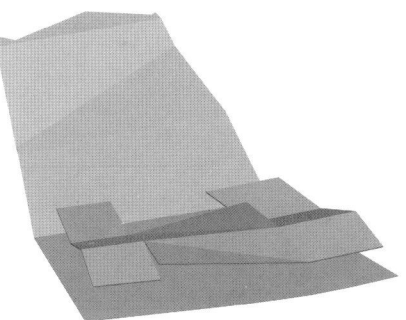

Canyon landscape = roof-scape

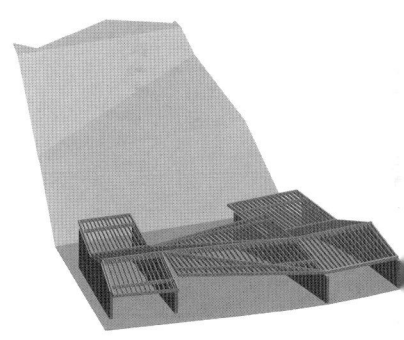

Wood canopy supported by blades

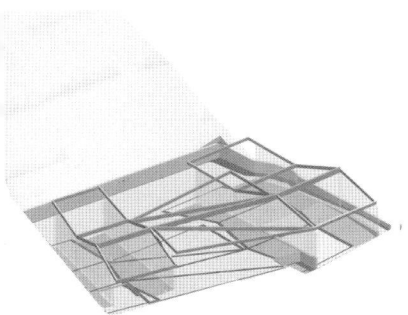

Corners are folded up to open main living space to light and landscape beyond

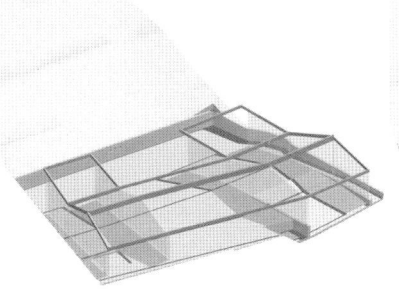

Beams hinge to fit site and roof section is subtracted to create open courtyard

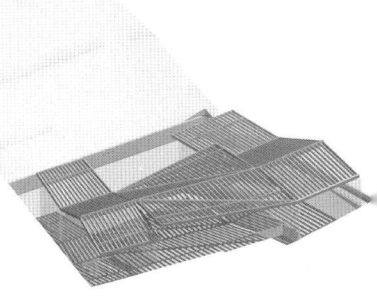

Full roofscape with all primary beams and secondary framing

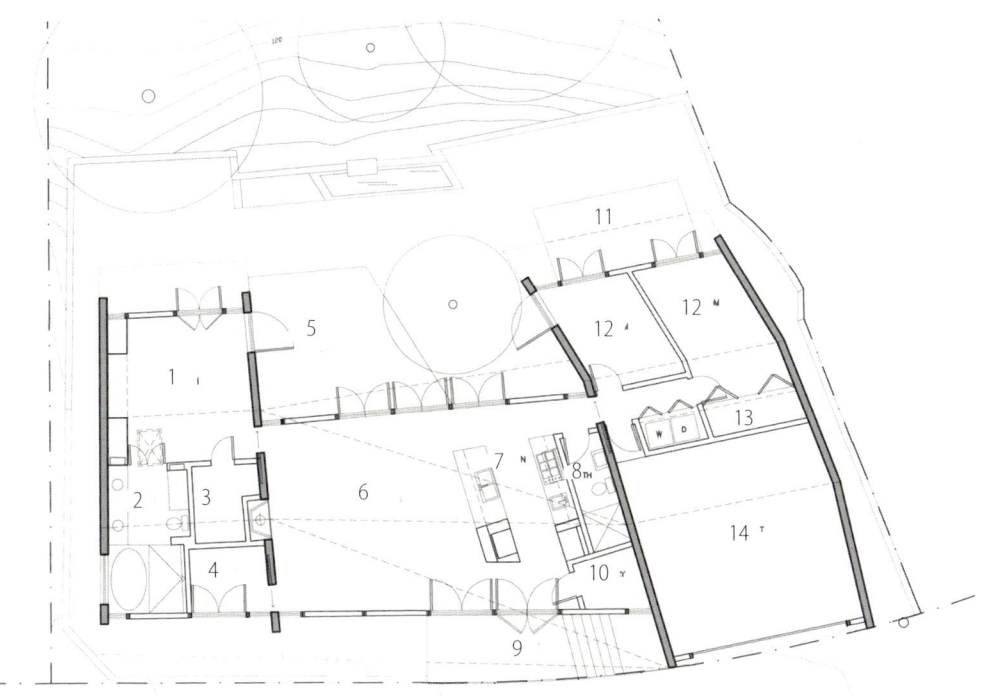

Ground floor plan

1. Master bedroom
2. Bath
3. Closet
4. Study
5. Patio
6. Living - dining
7. Kitchen
8. Bath
9. Entry
10. Pantry
11. Patio
12. Bedroom
13. Closet
14. Carport

West elevation

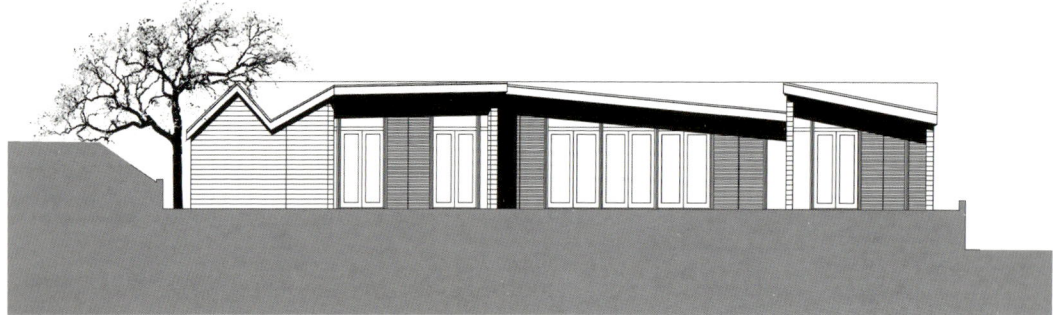
East elevation

The folds and cantilevers of the roof geometry are articulated to respond to specific site conditions: turned down at the street edge to create privacy; folded up above the bearing walls to gain light from the sides; and sloping up again at the rear of the site to open the interior spaces to the hillside through full-height glass panels.

Dieter Thiel

Bangert Studio and House

SCHOPFHEIM, GERMANY *Photographs: Klaus Frahm / Contur*

This German publisher's office on the slopes of an old orchard in the Black Forest is made of wood in the traditional way, but is entirely modern in design, technology and ecological awareness. The two buildings, while sharing the site with a house from the 50s, are completely divorced from it and each other and positioned in relation to some fine mature trees. They are an outstanding example of future-oriented design both ecologically and structurally. They also comply with the client's desire for clearly legible timber house architecture with variable lighting conditions, excellent indoor climatisation and perfect acoustics. The major of the two new structures (studio and library) comprises three different sized "wooden boxes" arranged in open plan so that, given the complete absence of partitions, the open cluster creates a room of great visual tension 17.6 meters long and with three different widths and heights. The other new cube, rising obliquely positioned at some distance from it on a 7.2 m2. floor plan functions as a two-storey guesthouse.

As opposed to conventional timber houses, its fundamental difference is that it has uncompromisingly materialized the idea of a building devoid of extra finishings such as cladding and lining. The system complied at once with the client's demand that individual cubes be prefabricated on a maximum scale to achieve the best possible quality of workmanship and the shortest possible in-situ installation time.

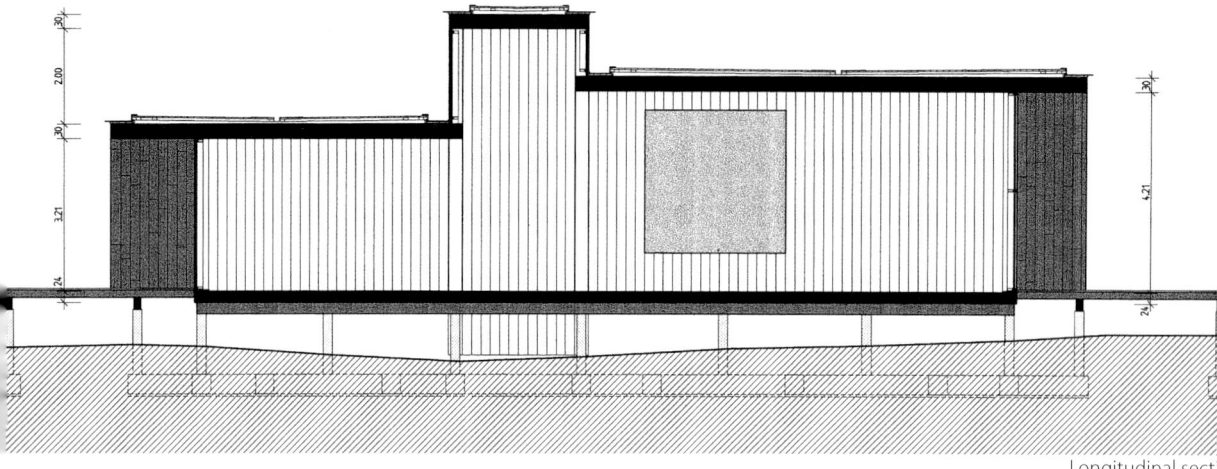

Longitudinal sect

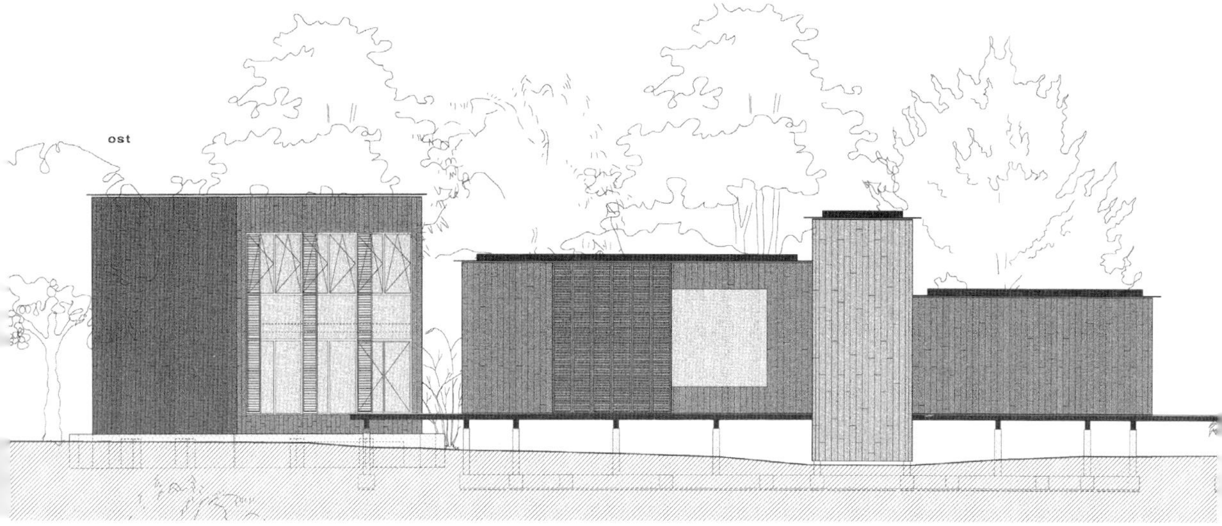

East elevation

The major of the two new structures (studio and library) comprises three different sized "wooden boxes" arranged in open plan so that, given the complete absence of partitions, the open cluster creates a room of great visual tension 17.6 meters long and with three different widths and heights.

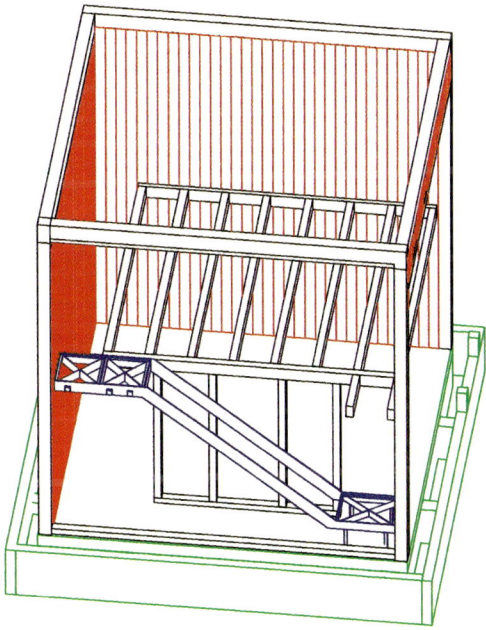

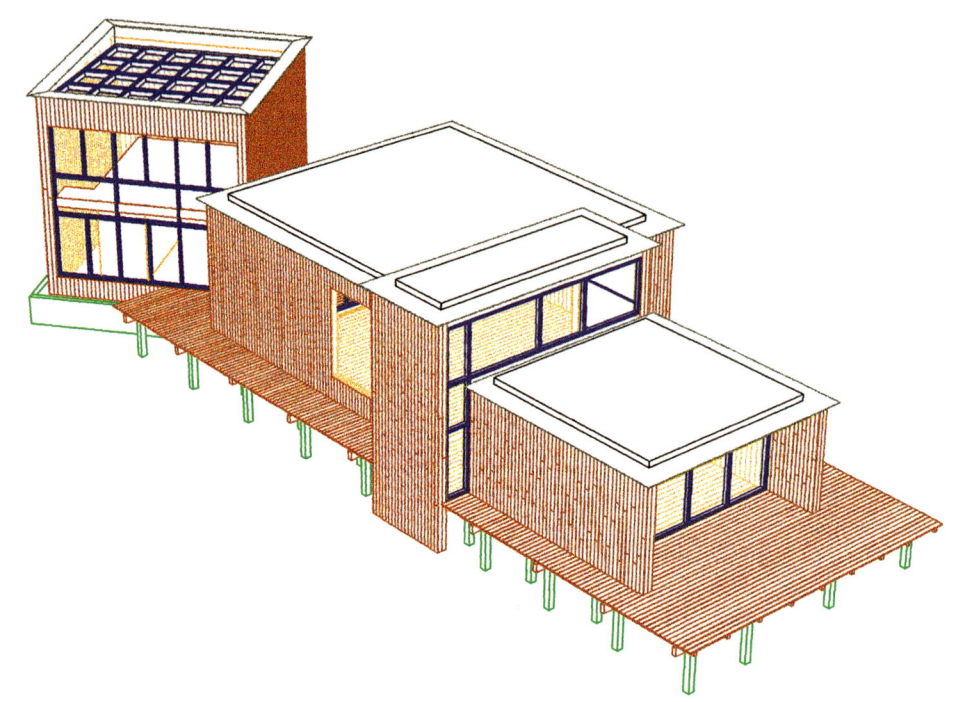

Daigo Ishii + Future-Scape

Cottage in Kawanishi

KAWANISHI, JAPAN *Photographs: Future Scape and Japan Architect*

This cottage is located in the region of Japan that receives the greatest amount of annual snowfall, which is sometimes as deep as four meters. At the same time, summer temperatures might soar as high as 38º C (100º F) and are usually accompanied by an uncomfortably high level of humidity. Such climatic conditions inevitably became determining forces in the design of this home in the woods.

Local architectural tradition necessarily formed the basis for the external shape of the building, especially the roof, with its sharp ridge and steep slope to prevent a dangerous accumulation of heavy snow. Furthermore, the ridge is exactly in the centerline of the roof to ensure an equal distribution on either side of snow. The overhang of the eaves has been kept as short as possible to ensure that as snow melts in the spring and piles up at the lower end of the roof plane, it will be well supported by the load-bearing walls of the structure.

Another determining factor in the shape of the cottage was the budget, with this simple rectangle occupying the largest possible volume. The wide, open spaces of the interior were needed to create a comfortable degree of air flow during the hot, humid summer months.

The end result of these combined functions is referred to by the architect as "Black Box, White Tube". The black box is the basic shape, and is plainly seen as such even from the inside, surrounding the negative spaces leftover from the "white tube". The white tube, enclosed in slip-boarded dividing walls, is a row of volumes housing the home's essential functions (bathrooms, bedrooms, kitchen, etc.). However, rather than being placed in a straight row, the restricted length of the house has resulted in a bent and jumbled "row" which guarantees the maximum degree of space for each function.

A traditional vernacular was used on the exterior in order to keep its external look in line with the other homes in the area and so as not to aesthetically compete with the surrounding beech woods. However, the impression changes radically on the inside, with an unexpected juxtaposition of shapes and tones in a purely contemporary idiom.

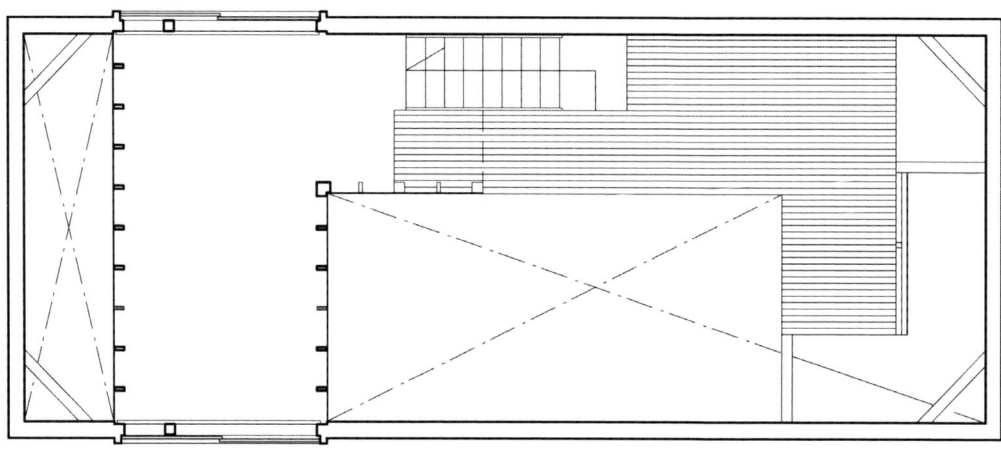

High floor plan

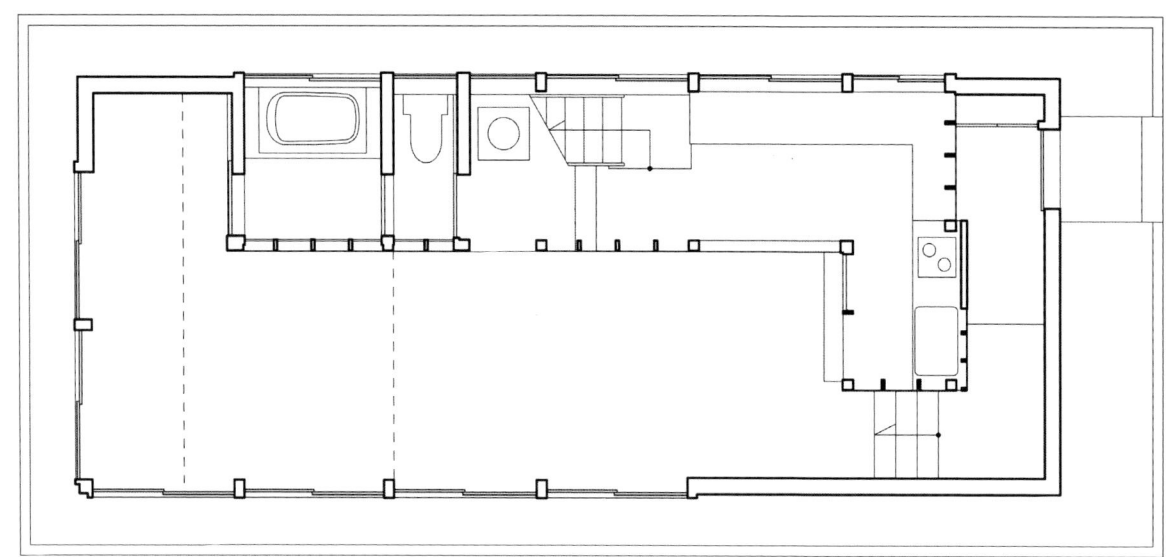

Ground floor plan

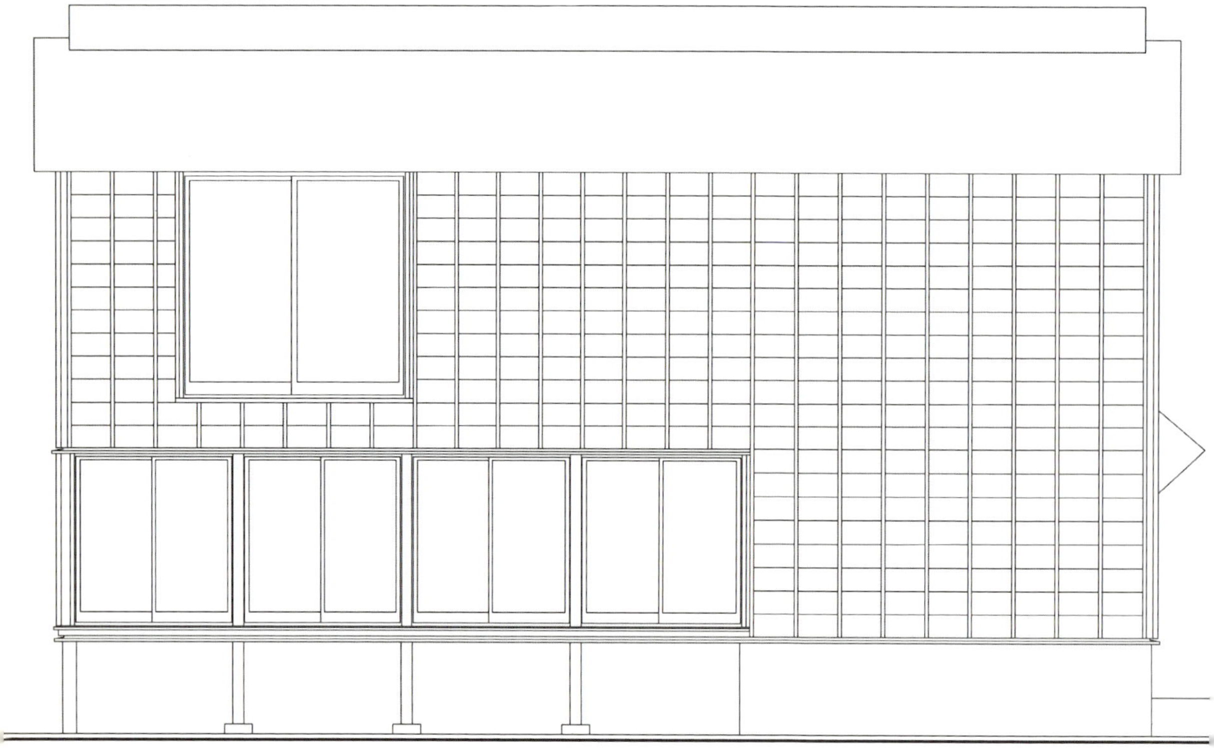

Longitudinal elevation

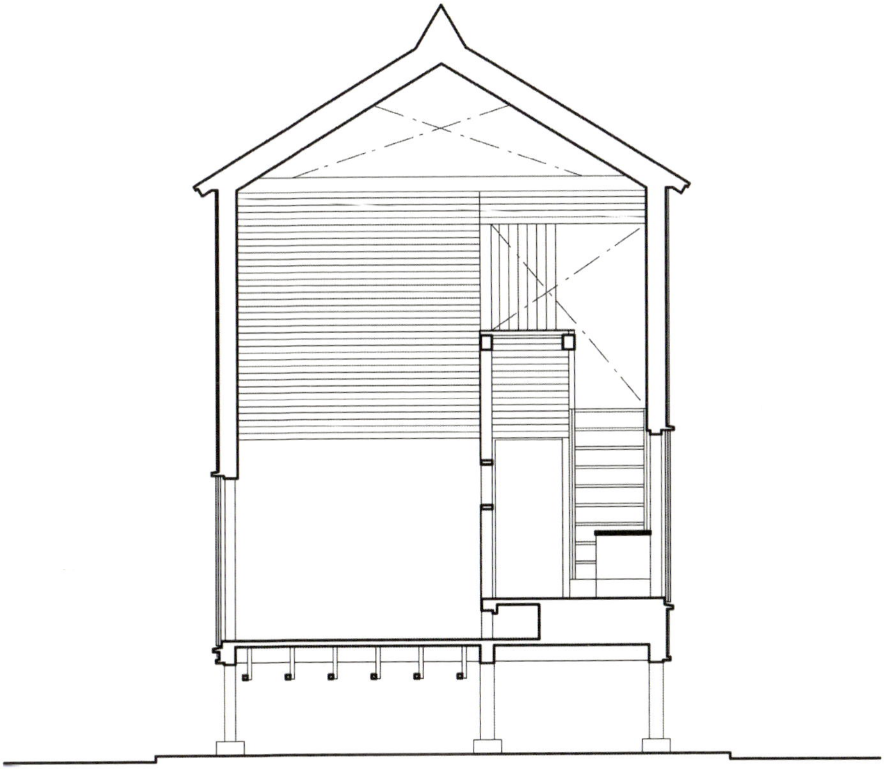

Cross section

Gap between the two volumes: Black Box and White Cube

Black Box

Maximum volume possible from budget

Local know-how for withstanding heavy snow

Realization and adjustment

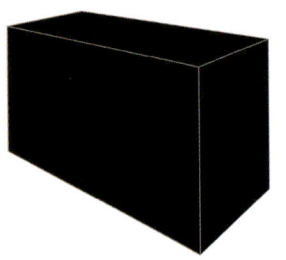
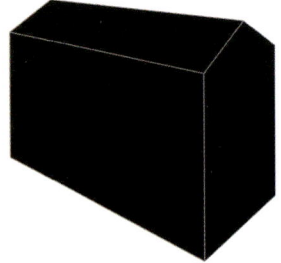
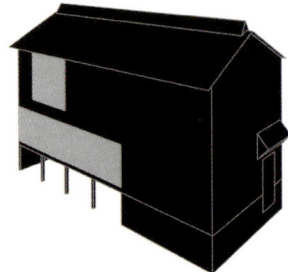

White Tube

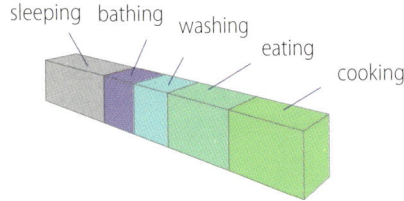
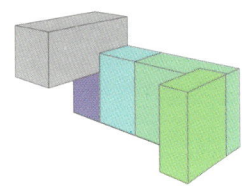
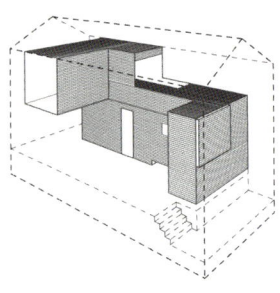

Essential living functions

Bent by the restriction of Black Box

Realization and adjustment

A traditional vernacular was used on the exterior in order to keep its external look in line with the other homes in the area and so as not to aesthetically compete with the surrounding beech woods. However, the impression changes radically on the inside, with an unexpected juxtaposition of shapes and tones in a purely contemporary idiom.

Smiths Architects

Smith McLain Cabin

Castle Rock, Colorado, USA

Photographs: Smiths Architects

As a project the 186 sqft (17.3 m2) cabin represents two urban dwellers needs to escape the city. In a subdivided cattle ranch of 40 acre plots overlooking the Sangre De Cristo mountain range, the cabin is a modern day settlers claim. Perched on an outcropping of rocks at 9,800 feet it is an amalgam of the windblown Bristlecone pine and the tectonics of the early settlers cabins both indigenous to the area.

The cabin's skin alternately is tongue-and-groove cedar or 5/8" exterior plywood with 1x4 cedar slatting over 2x2 cedar battens. The design recalls the horizontal lines in the body of settlers cabins and the vertical quality of board and batten frequently used in the gable. Battens are installed directly behind 2x4 studs concealing plywood joints and linking vertically to roof joists. This configuration reveals the inner construction of studs spaced at 16" on center and as interrupted by king and trimmer studs at window and door openings. Programatically the screen allows for security shutters over windows and escape from the heat of mid-day sun.

The varying pitches and attenuated extensions of the roof form recall the Bristlecone as an expression of wind. Roof pitches respond to the program needs of awning at the entry and shelter/transition at the living area/ deck passage. The different heights set a heirarchy between the service (kitchen/ mud-room) side and the living area side. Galvanized corrugated metal roofing and details both inside and out assure longevity and link to the indigenous vocabulary of "ranch".

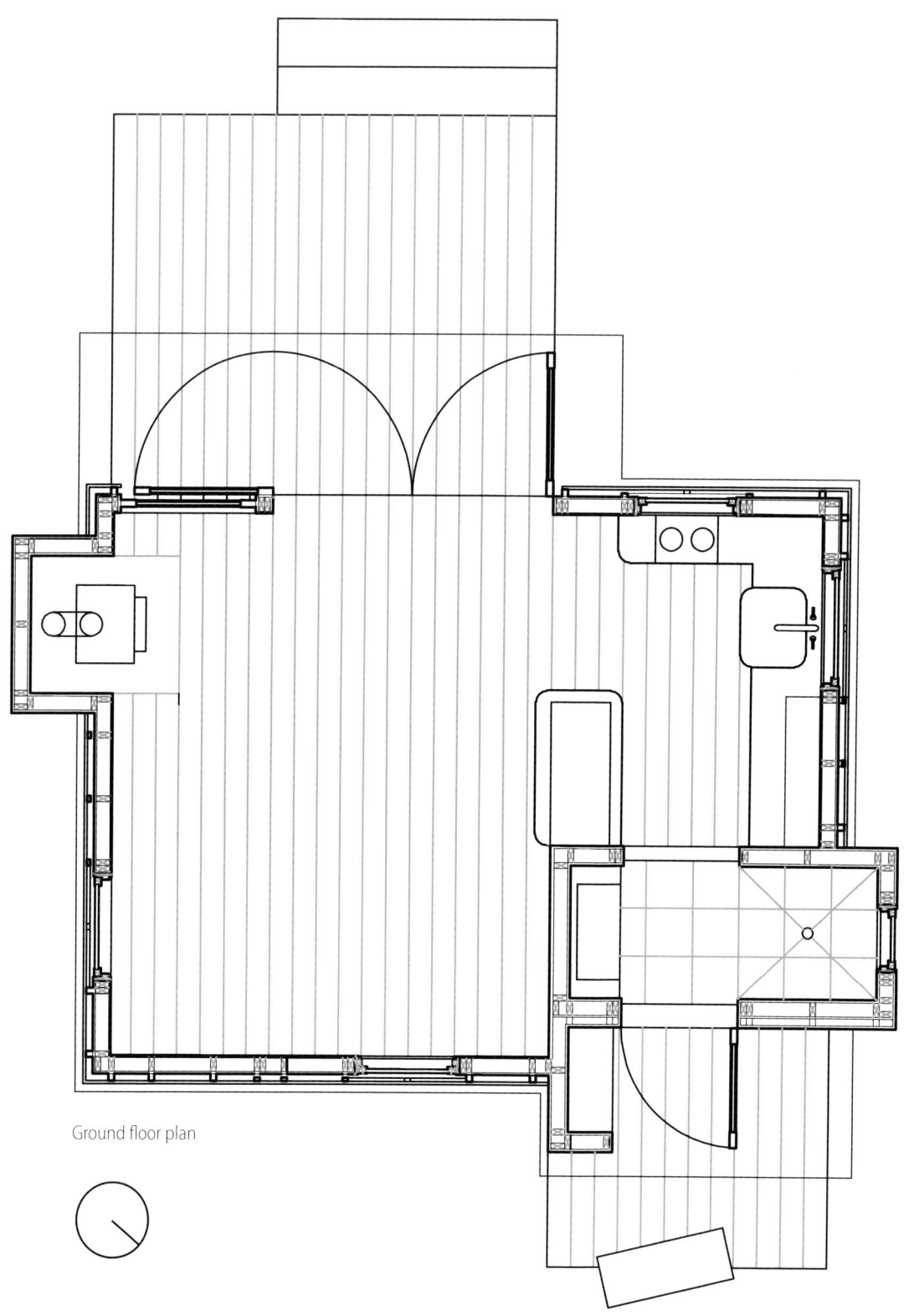

Ground floor plan

South elevation

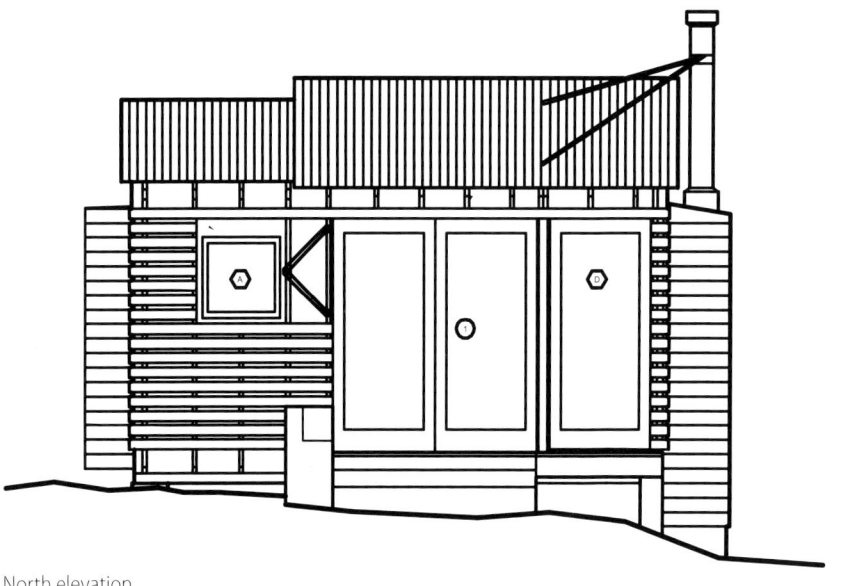
North elevation

West elevation

East elevation

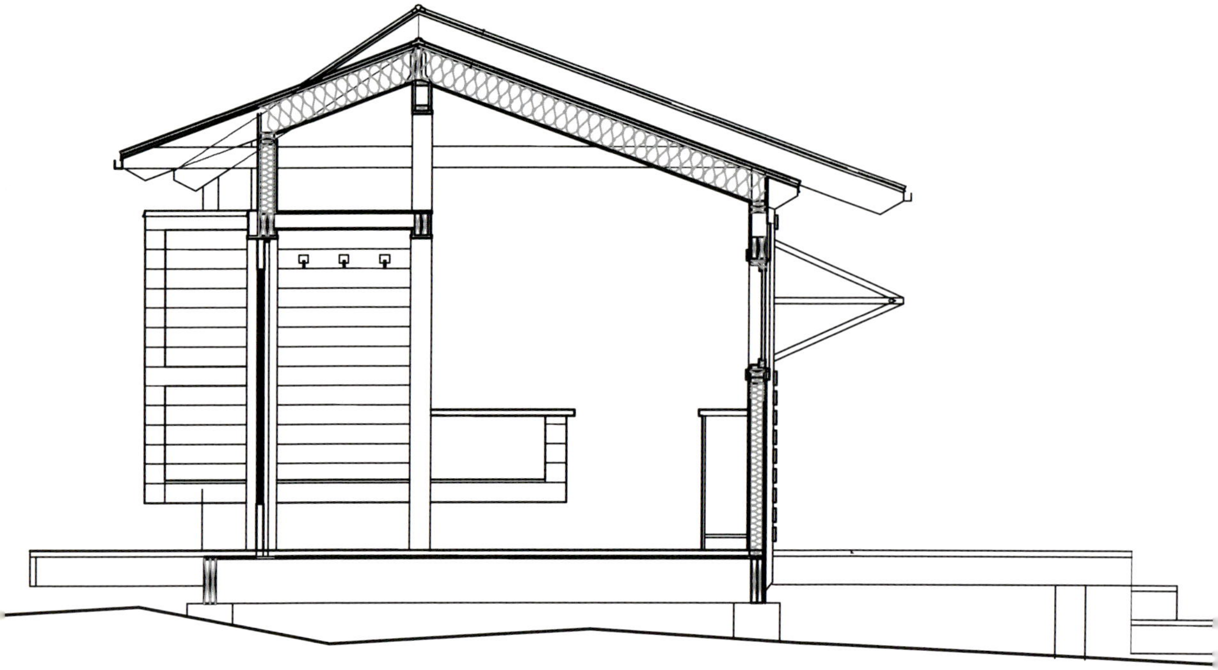

West-East section

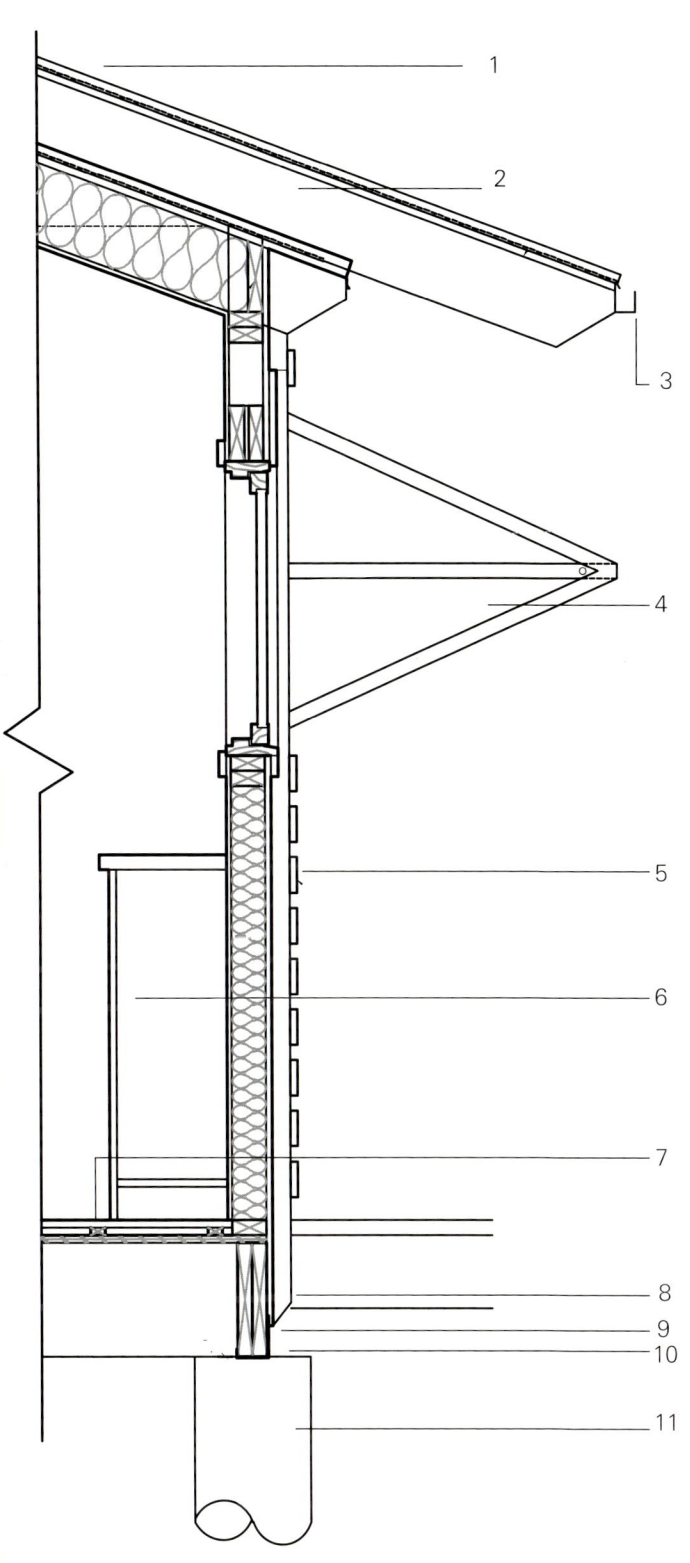

Wall Section

1. Corrugated metal roof (2″ corrugations) on 30# felt on ¾″ plywood deck, R-30 insulation, plywood interior
2. Cedar boards in lieu of plywood at underside of exposed leaves
3. Custom 2-1/2″ x 2-1/2″ galvanized gutter and drip edge
4. Steel shutter support
5. 1x4 cedar slating on 2x2 cedar battens on 5/8″ exterior plywood (dark stain) 2x4 studs w/ R-13 batt insulation
6. Built-in cabinets of cedar boards and 2x4s, galvanized hinges and pulls
7. 3/4″ x 6″ character marked ash wood floor on 1x2 sleepers
8. 450 cut at base of battens corresponds to b.o. plywood
9. Bottom of plywood
10. Galvanized metal base wrap
11. Concrete pier

The different heights set a heirarchy between the service (kitchen/ mud-room) side and the living area side).

José Cruz Ovalle

House in Santo Domingo

ROCAS DE SANTO DOMINGO, CHILE *Fotografías: Juan Purcell*

This dwelling located on a slope facing the sea is raised above the land on reinforced concrete slabs and built entirely in wood, thus providing an effective and aesthetic solution to the problem of damp that is often found in coastal areas.

In this building of 350 sqm on a plot of 1,135 sqm the architects attempted to configure a space "illuminated" by the surrounding landscape and not simply dominated by it, as often happens in houses located on the seafront. The seascape usually steals the interior space by dissipating it toward the horizon in a single direction. To respond to this presence, the architects invented the "counter-view", which seeks its power in the maximum expansion of a space that opens its depth in multiple directions. This is achieved by rotating the house around a courtyard that is open to the sea and sheltered from the prevailing winds, in order to form a double interior. This rotation partly accommodates the slope of the land by means of the different horizontal levels of the floor, as a way of multiplying the vertical lines in order to create the oblique depths that measure and graduate the characteristic "up" and "down" relationship of a sloping site.

The "counterview" is thus here the abstraction that proposes an oriented but not directed interior and that balances the eloquence of the landscape by means of a space developed in different directions that relates proximity and distance. This exercise allows the surrounding dual elements (the land and its slope, the neighbouring houses and their gardens, the extension of the beach and the reef, the distance of the sea and the horizon…) to illuminate the interior of this house without dominating it.

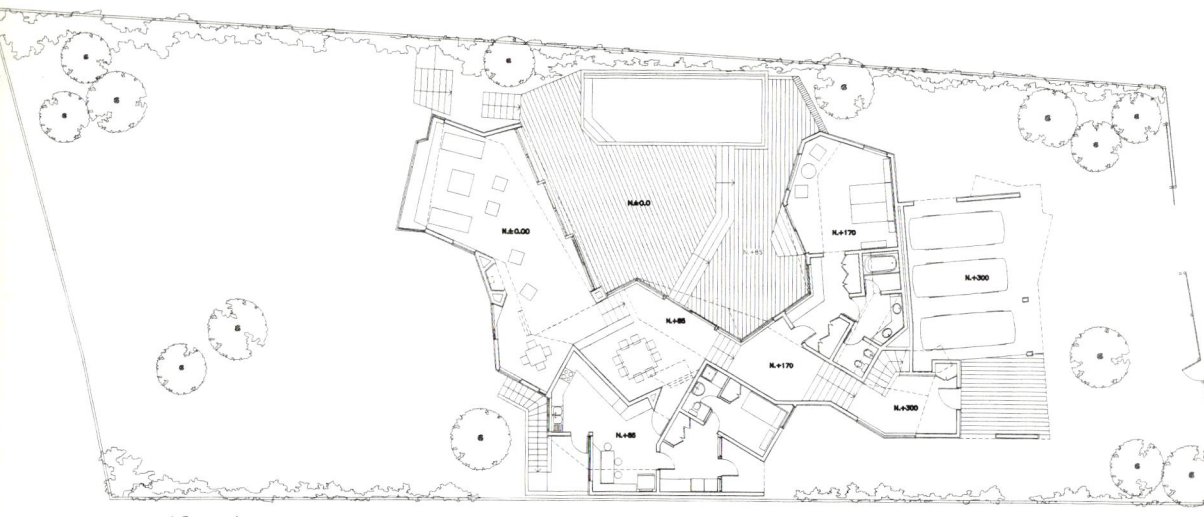

Ground floor plan

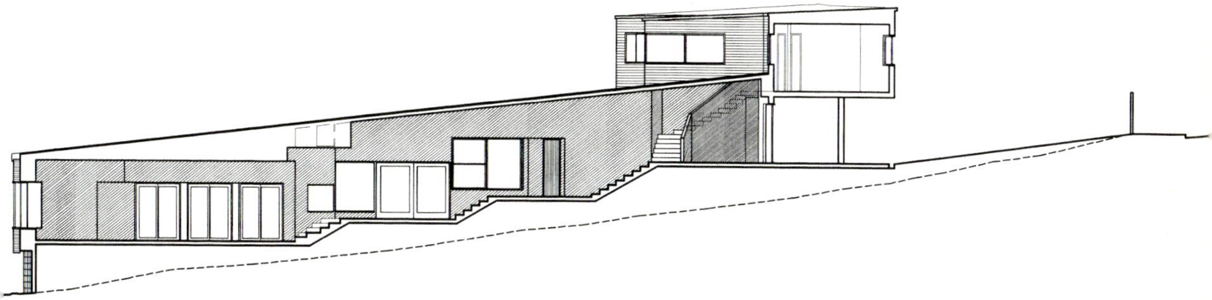

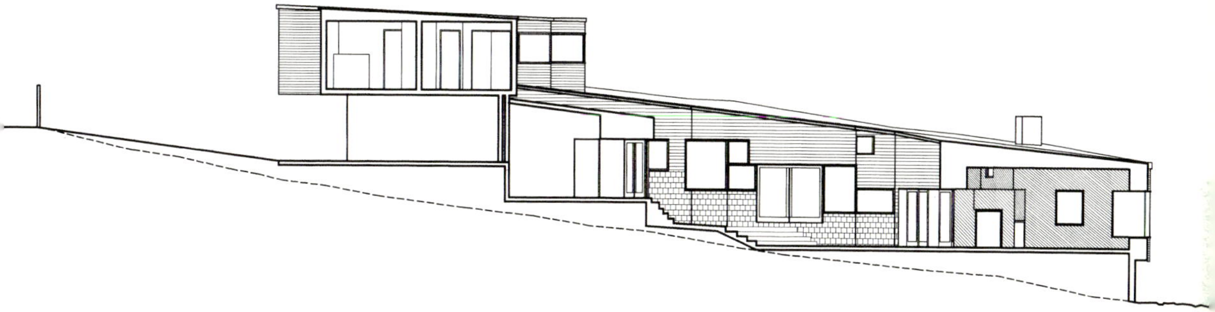

Longitudinal sections

Taylor Smyth Architects

Sunset Cabin

Lake Simcoe, Canada   *Photographs: Ben Rahn / A-Frame Inc. & Taylor Smyth*

Since the clients entertain up to 15 overnight visitors at a time during the summer at their family cottage on Lake Simcoe, their personal privacy is a prime concern, for which they requested a separate sleeping cabin for their personal use. Their primary requirement was to be able to lie in bed and watch the sunset.

The project consists of a single 275 sqft (25.5m2) room. All components are built in, including the bed and a wall of storage cabinets on either side. The floor of the cabin extends outside towards the lake to become a deck with access to an outdoor shower enclosed by a cedar screen. The cabin is fabricated of clear cedar for window frames, doors and cladding. The cedar is untreated, gradually turning silver and blending the structure into the landscape. All interior surfaces are birch veneer plywood panels - floors, back wall and ceiling and storage, so no repainting is required. The cabin was first constructed in a parking lot in Toronto over a period of 4 weeks by a group of craftsmen who usually build furniture. This allowed for details to be worked out precisely and all the components to be pre-fabricated. These were numbered, disassembled and reconstructed on site in just 10 days. Prefabrication reduced costs by an estimated 30% by decreasing construction time and simplifying the difficulties of working at a remote, sloping site, and hence reduced labor costs. Three walls of the cabin are floor to ceiling glass, wrapped by an exterior horizontal cedar screen on two sides for privacy and sun shading. A large cut-out in the screen is carefully located to provide spectacular views of the setting sun from the bed. Gaps between the individual members of the screen increase arbitrarily as the cabin gets closer to the lake, framing snapshots of random, seemingly abstract compositions of vegetation, lake and sky. The clients had potentially conflicting requirements for maximum views and openness, yet combined with privacy from the main cottage. The density of the screen gradually diminishes as it moves away from the main cottage. The screen obscures views in, while enabling views out. Practical requirements dictated configuration in the case of the long glass wall that angles away from the outer cedar screen to allow space to wash the windows. The result is a fascinating play of light on the glass. The cabin is located on an existing level piece of ground, chosen both for its views and to avoid the need to remove any trees. It is supported on 2 steel beams resting on 4 concrete caissons. This allows the cabin to rest lightly on the site, with minimal disruption to vegetation. A Green Roof, planted with sedums and herbs, allows the cabin to blend into the landscape due to the visibility of the roof from the main cottage at the top of the hill. Passive Energy Saving Measures have also been incorporated: the exterior cedar screen provides sun shading, while doors at each end capitalize on lake breezes and provide cross ventilation.

▶ © Ben Rahn / A-Frame Inc.

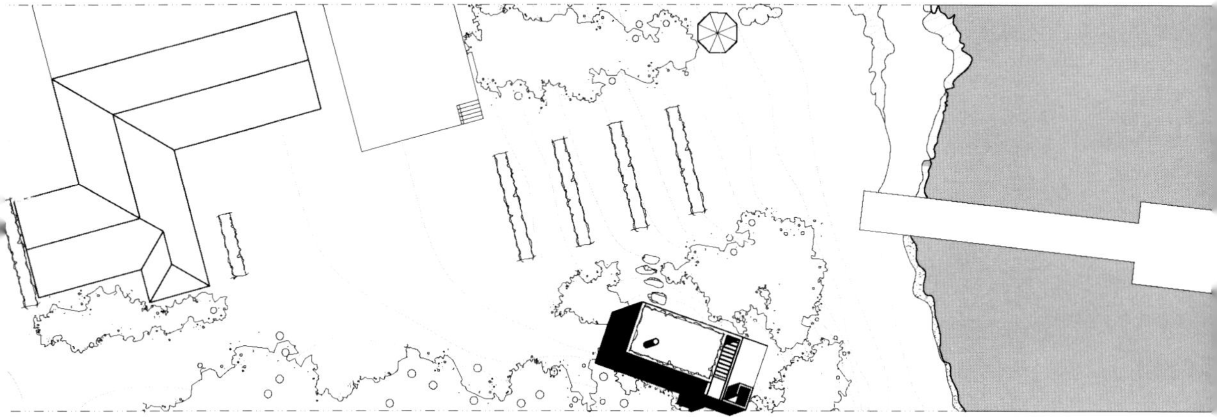

Site plan

© Ben Rahn / A-Frame

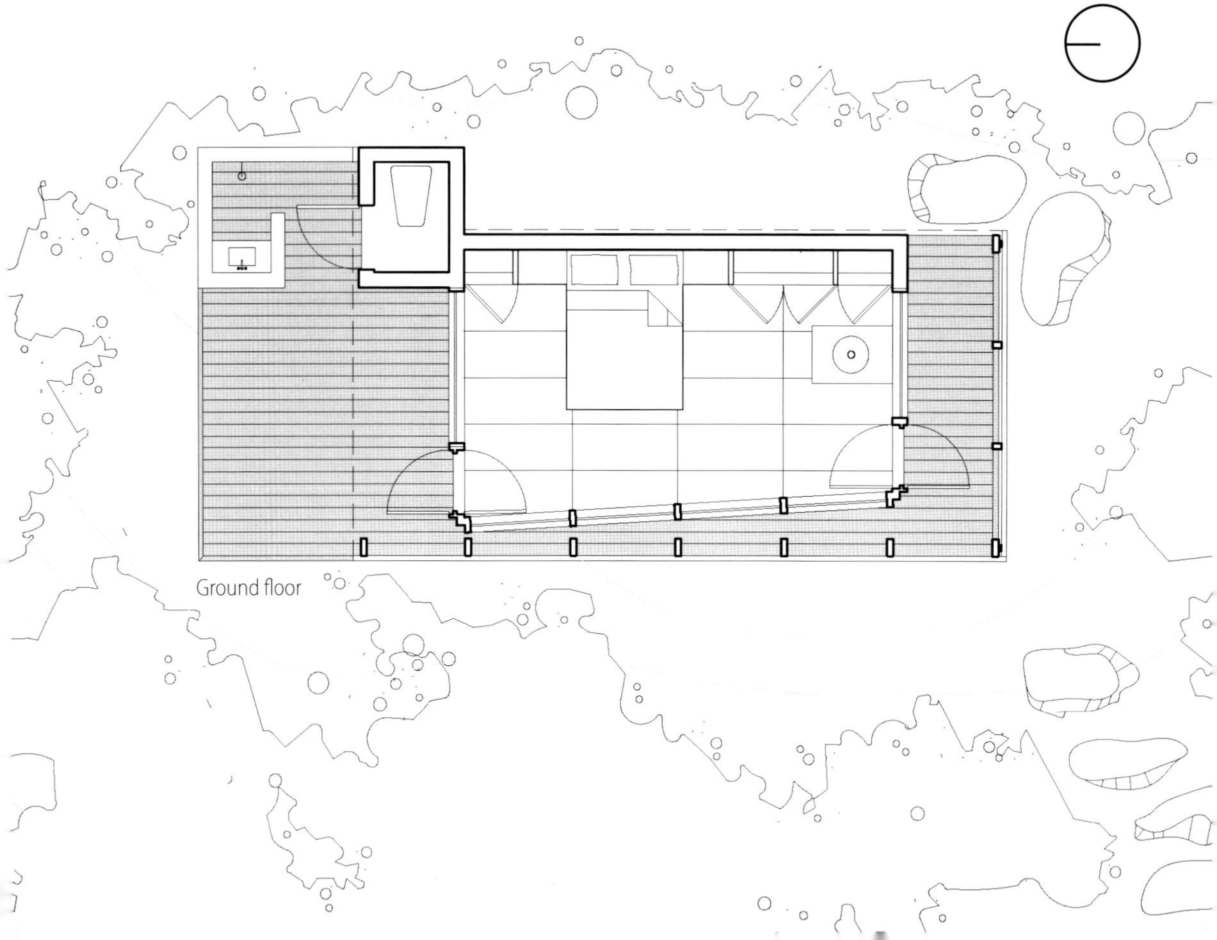

Ground floor

© Ben Rahn / A-Frame Inc.

© Ben Rahn / A-Frame Inc.

© Taylor Smyth

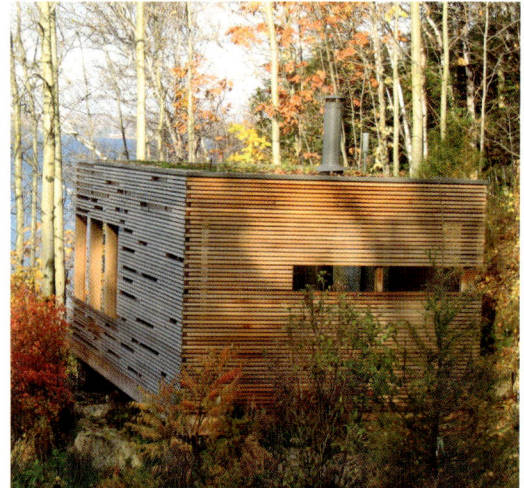

The cabin is located on an existing level piece of ground, chosen both for its views and to avoid the need to remove any trees. It is supported on 2 steel beams resting on 4 concrete caissons. This allows the cabin to rest lightly on the site, with minimal disruption to vegetation.

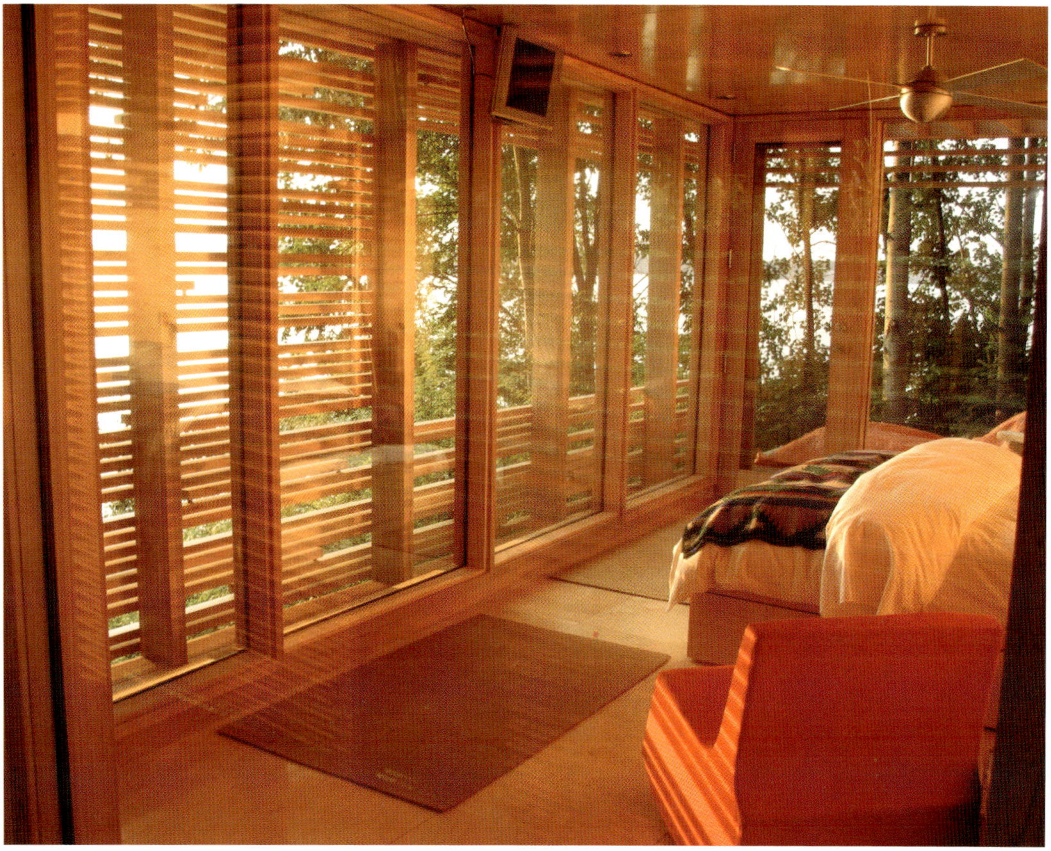

▼ © Ben Rahn / A-Frame Inc.

▲ © Taylor Smyth

Practical requirements dictated configuration in the case of the long glass wall that angles away from the outer cedar screen to allow space to wash the windows. The result is a fascinating play of light on the glass.

© Ben Rahn / A-Frame Inc.

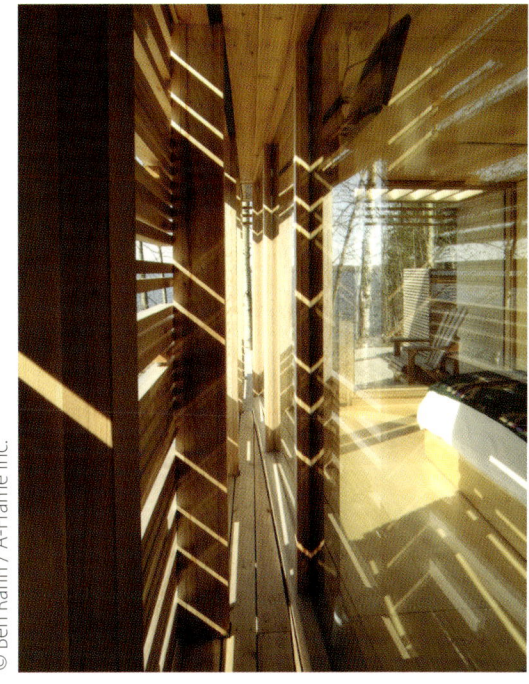

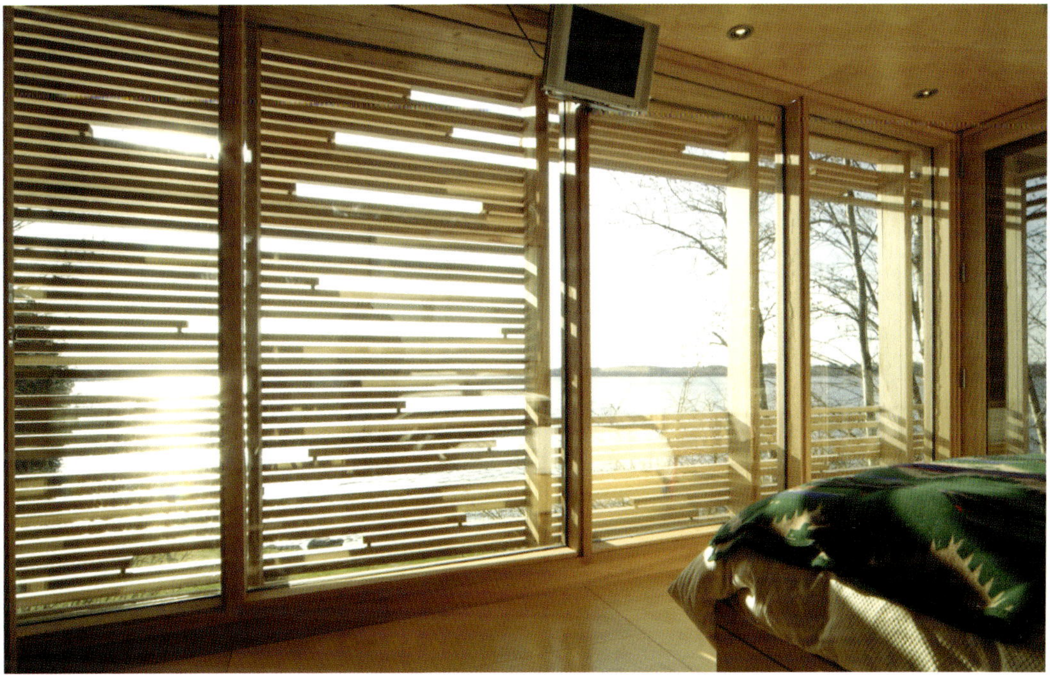

▼▲ © Ben Rahn / A-Frame Inc.

Nendo

Drawer-House

MEJIRO, TOKYO, JAPAN *Photographs: Nacása & Partners*

The constant ebb and flow between action and rest, between a multifunctional cluttered space, and the restful reduction of a room's accessories to the minimum seems particularly relevant in city like Tokyo. The inspiration for Drawer House, as its name expresses, is the magic of concealing our plethora of miscellaneous objects behind closed screens or "drawers", keeping them for later. All the range of household functions – Tables, beds, shelves, partitions and whole rooms can be drawn out when they are wanted. The rest of the time, their existence can be temporarily forgotten. Basic functions, like the kitchen and the bathroom, are neatly hidden behind closed doors, Even the main access to the house or the openings onto the stairs are only signified by a discreet opening mechanism, so the home becomes a conjuring trick to which only the permanent inhabitants know the secret.

The building is distributed on three floors. The ground floor has a total surface area of 63.79m2; the first floor above is only 54.48 m2, as it leaves some free space for a glass floor terrace. With 44.24 m2, the basement is somewhat smaller still.

The site has been separated from the street by a fence of timber studs the whole height of the building. Sunshine filters through the studs and penetrates the almost entirely glass façade, shedding a stripy pattern of light on the slate floor downstairs; The opposite end of this room is brightly lit through the glass floor of the terrace upstairs. The walls and all the drawers and doors where all the accessories are waiting, are made of white ash plywood stained with natural white oil, throughout the house. The upstairs floor is oak. In the basement, the pale sandstone floor lightens a potentially oppressive space. The hidden interiors of all the drawers, such as bookshelves, beds, or other spaces, are finished in dark Japanese Liden plywood, starkly illustrating the opposition between visible and invisible.

The architects responsible for this solution pride themselves in their flexible approach to projects. The name of the firm, Nendo, means clay in Japanese. Oki Sato (of Nendo's seven-man design team), won the Good Design Award 2004.

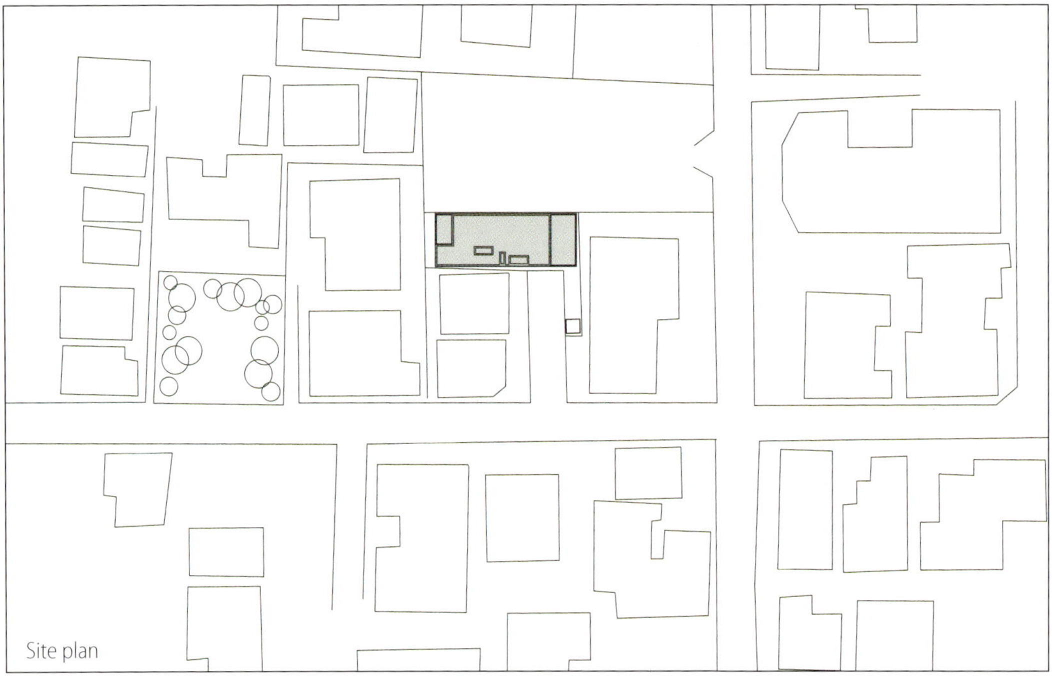

Site plan

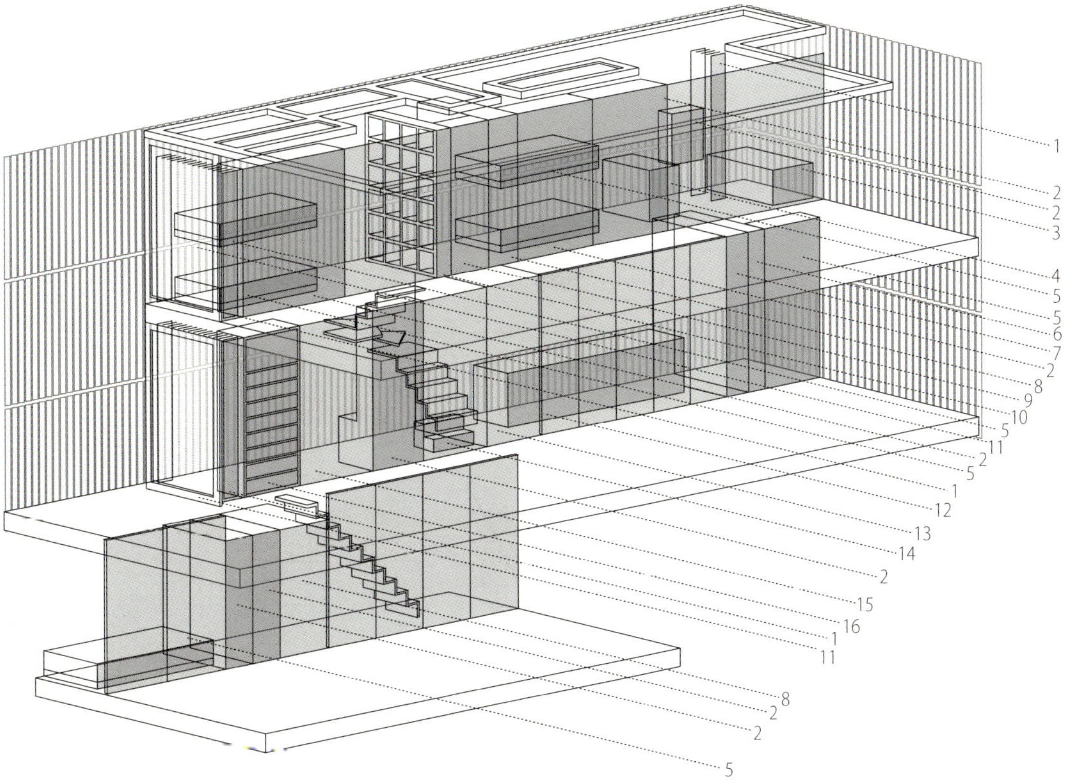

1. Curtain	9. Desk + chair
2. Storage	10. Bookshelf
3. Bath	11. Window
4. Toilet	12. Kitchen
5. Bed	13. Lavatory
6. Cupboard	14. Stairs
7. TV	15. Entrance
8. Closet	16. Cloak

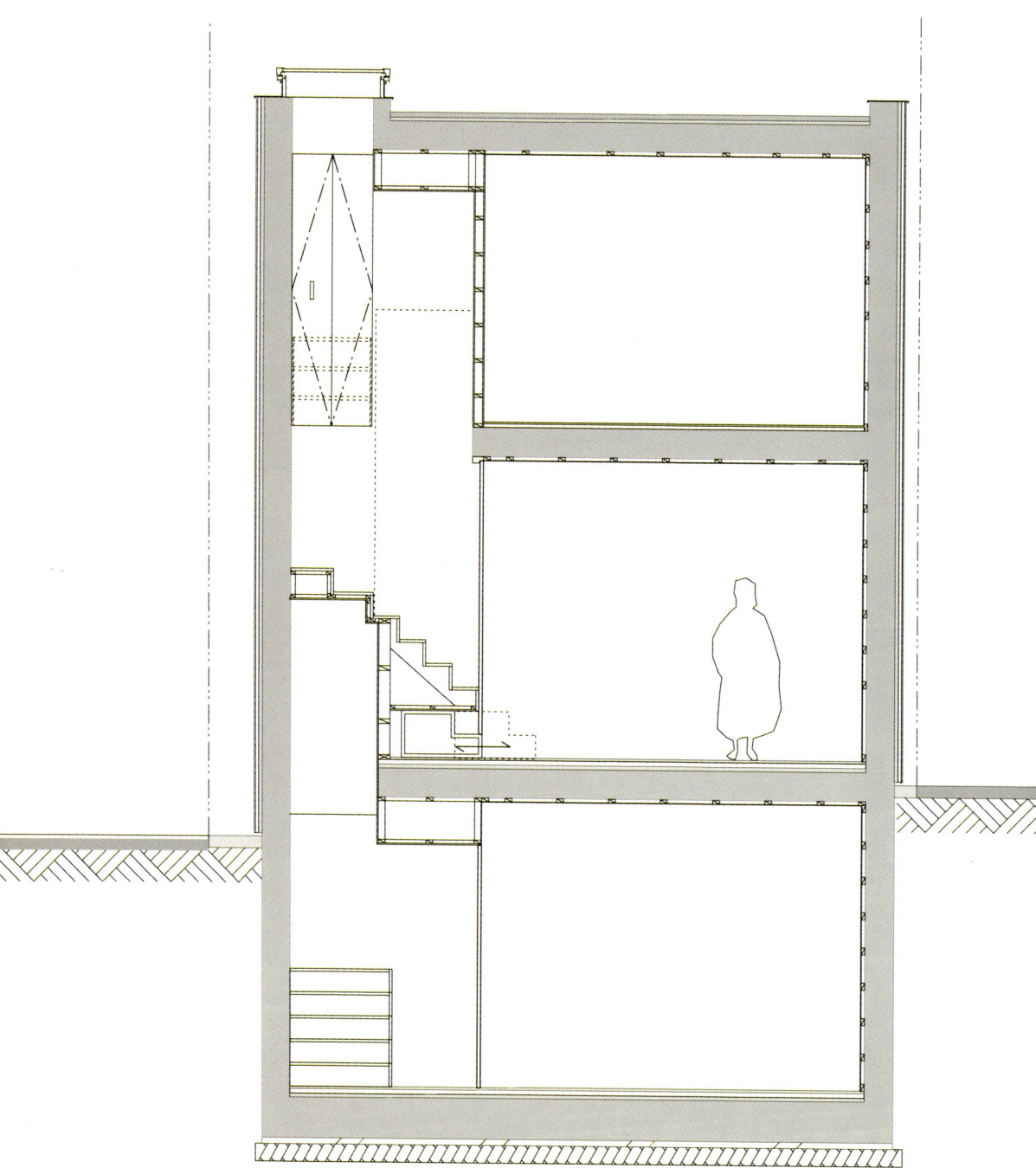

Pierre Thibault

Beaver's Lake Refuge

GRANDES-PILES, QUÉBEC, CANADA *Photographs: Alain Laforest*

The program was for a four-season refuge large enough to accommodate family and friends and serve as a permanent residence. The 4000-square-foot (371.61 sqm) project had to contain three bedrooms and facilities, a workroom, an office and large living spaces.

The site, Beaver Lake, is an entrancing environment located in the heart of a forest that features no visible trace of man's presence. The lake, surrounded by a soothing but penetrating landscape, is dotted with beaver dams. Dark trunks float on the surface of the water. Around the lake, trees are gnawed and stripped; unadorned silhouettes of trees emit a forceful presence that cannot be overlooked. Moss covers giant boulders and branches strewn over the forest floor seem like part of an unfinished painting. The environmental after effects of the natural 'builders' for whom the lake was named became the model behind the design concept, guiding the project's development.

The organizational design logically followed the shoreline and the living spaces were integrated accordingly. Made up of four distinct blocks, the house is linked by a wall of logs delineating a corridor - a backbone, or ballast - to the villa. Four roofs appear to float over these blocks like giant parasols, held in place by slanted wooden poles that echo and meld into the surrounding landscape.

Fragmenting the volume made it possible to size each block for height, width and depth according to the function it would house and the desired spatial sequence. Scrupulously studied in this way, these elements were thereby able to afford majestic heights in the main living area and to provide intimate bedrooms and a warm kitchen with cubic proportions.

Fragmentation also allowed orienting each block for the appropriate natural lighting and for specific visual pleasure. This flexibility allowed for the creation of a wide variety of spaces perfectly adapted to their use.

Permeability between the interior and the exterior rapidly became an important part of the project. Inside, trees become columns that vertically intersect both living spaces and corridor, giving rise to a dialogue between the rational logic of the villa and nature's organic counterpart. Outside, wooden floors reach out to the lake and become a terrace, met by the outer columns, which mirror the surrounding trees. Roofs angle toward the sky.

The organizational design logically followed the shoreline and the living spaces were integrated accordingly. Made up of four distinct blocks, the house is linked by a wall of logs delineating a corridor - a backbone, or ballast - to the villa.

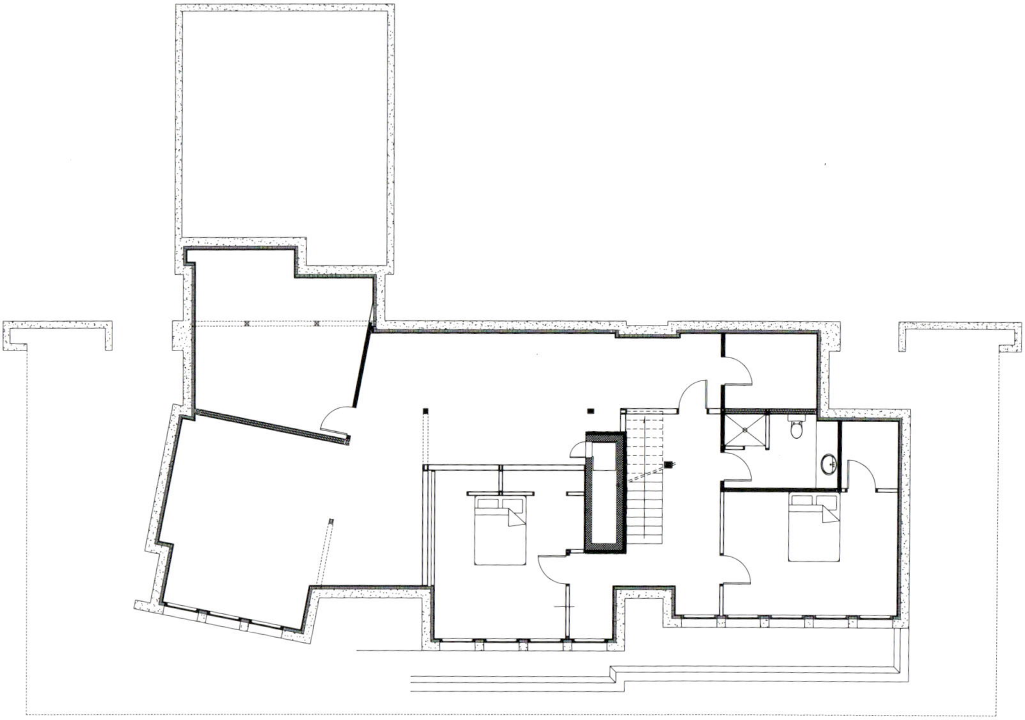

Basement floor plan

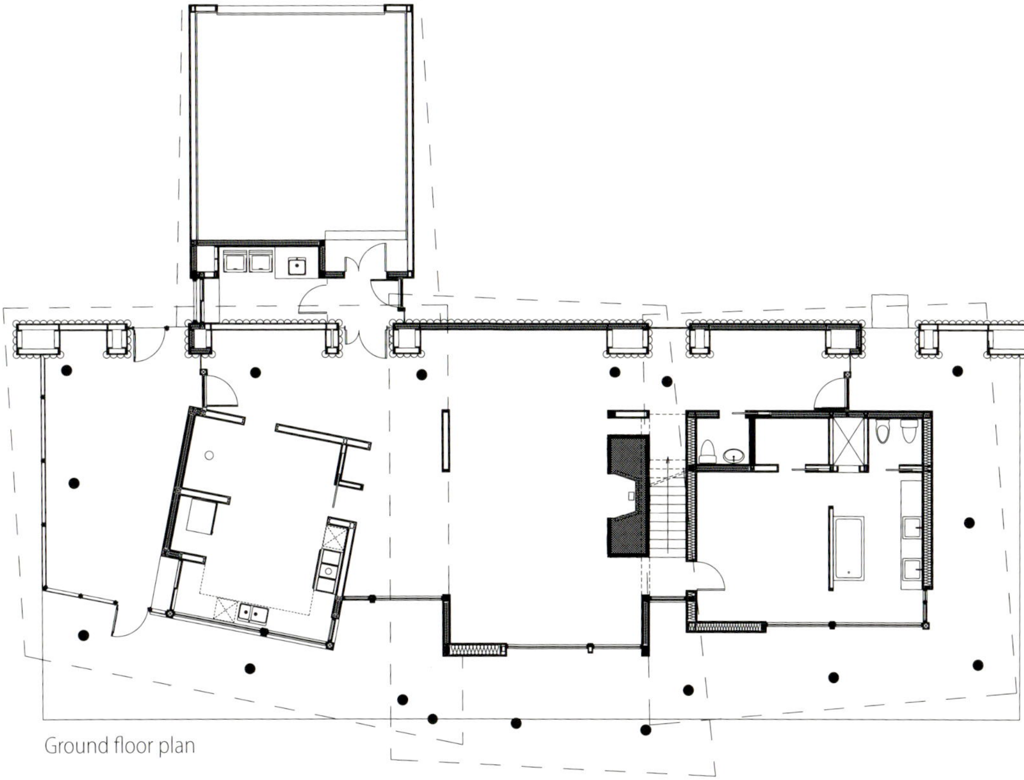

Ground floor plan

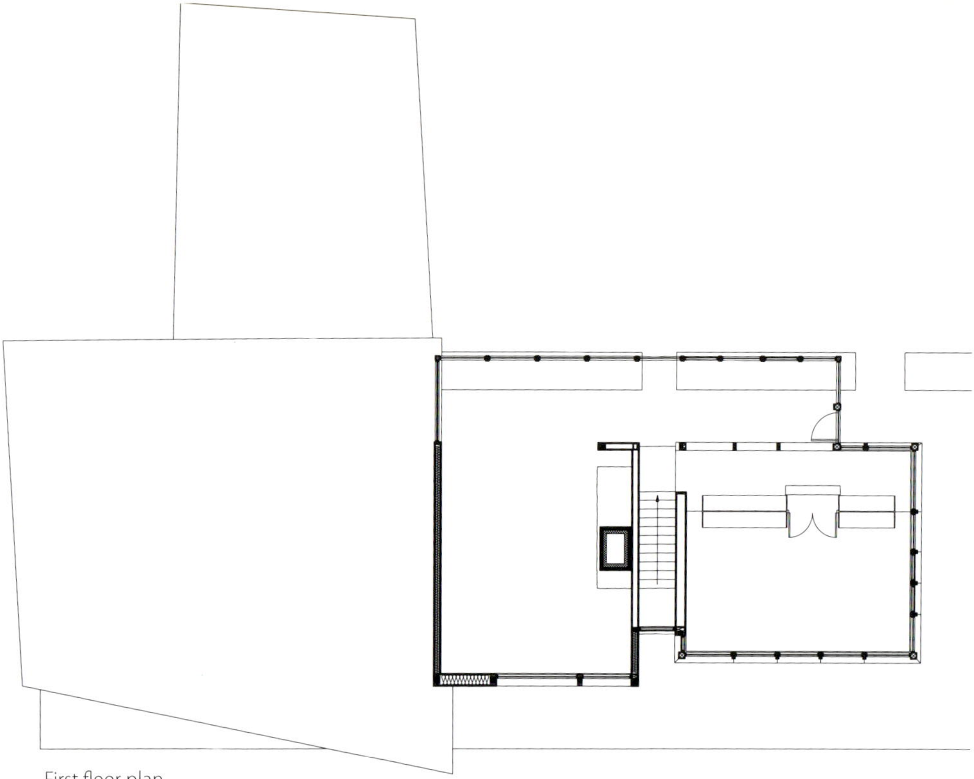

First floor plan

The villa is an extension of its environment, wide and generous at times, closed and careful at others, offering a lifestyle that incorporates nature in its very essence, melding the inside and the outside into one.

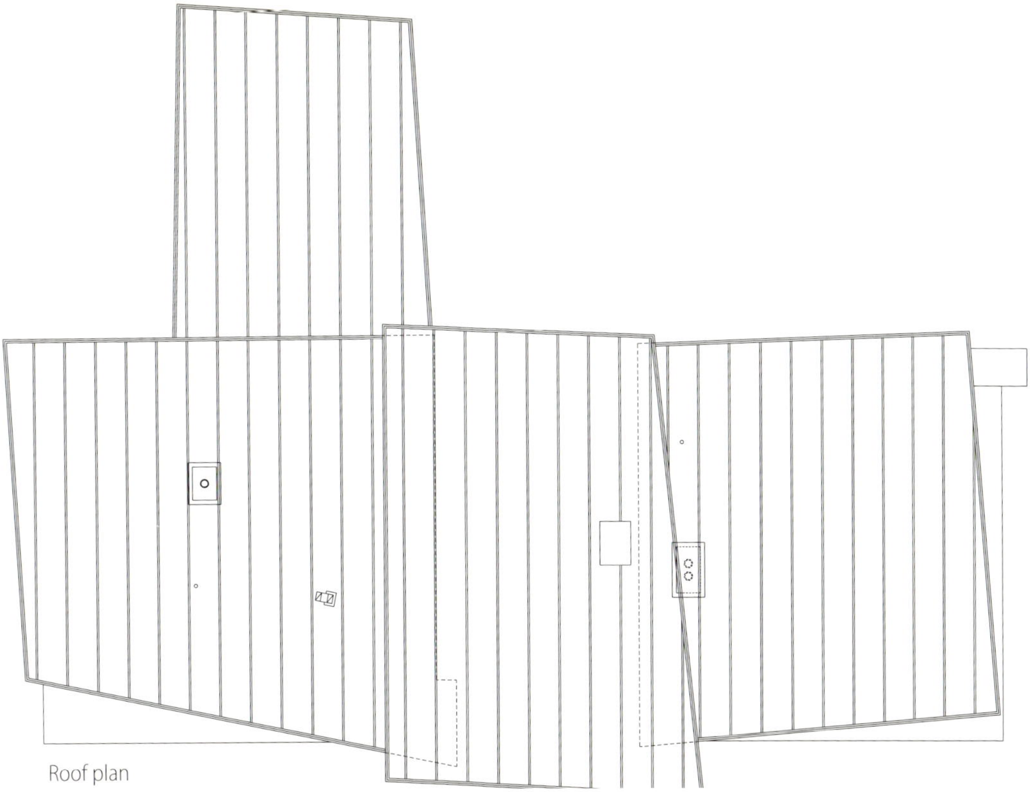

Roof plan

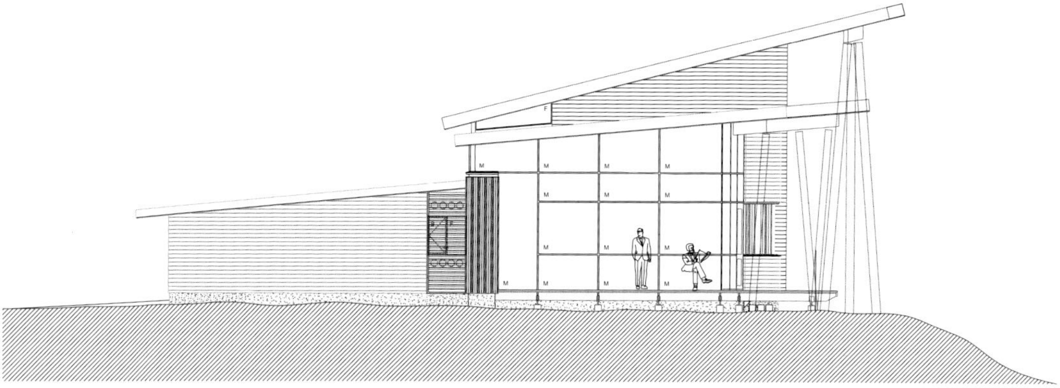

North elevation

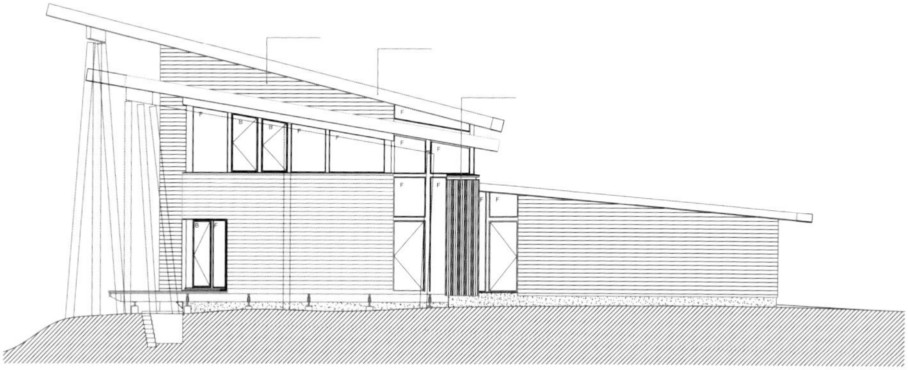

South elevation

West elevation

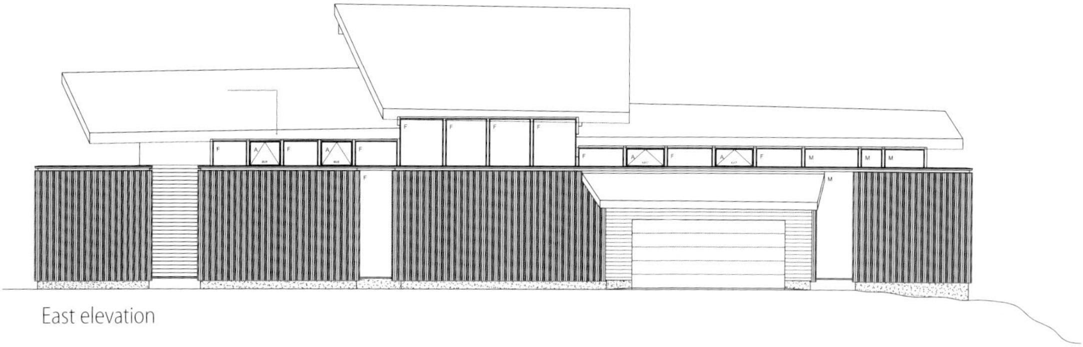

East elevation

Cesare Leonardi

Mescoli-Goich House

MODENA, ITALY *Photographs: Cesare Leonardi*

The architect decided to erase any past 'memory' of interior design so as to be free to explore the potential of a material that had aroused his curiosity - the formwork or shuttering panels used for concrete wall construction. There was also an initial condition: all designs had to be based on a single panel, its multiples or fractions, in order to work within a well-defined boundary. The ground rules allowed the use of only one material, one thickness (2.7 cm), one width, one finish, one color (a protective yellow varnish), five standard lengths (100, 150, 200, 250 and 300 cm), the screws necessary to hold an object together, and wheels to move it around. The goal was to produce a 'solid', by cutting and assembling panel pieces ready for storage and shipping. Everything was produced on the same CAD-laser cutter.

Once the first few shelves, beds and tables moved beyond the design stages, a further requirement became evident: the need to avoid waste when cutting a single panel into the components of an item of furniture.

As a result, the architect began to design objects by tracing their outlines directly onto the panel. Edges were traced flush against one another, and the complementary backs and support brackets, the one-piece seat, and the castor supports were carved from places that would not compromise the object's stability. The result was a small armchair whose sides, seat and backrest consist of pieces so composed as to enable them to develop formally through changes in the original configuration.

The solidification of the idea in ever new forms may arise from the recall of an elementary primal design, perhaps a mental archetype of a repressed activity, a 'memory' erased by many potential designs which demand that they as well as the archetypes be reviewed and, more often than not, that the limitations accumulated in the course of events be overcome. The architect's involvement in these 'metamorphoses' was a definite though unconscious choice of methodology.

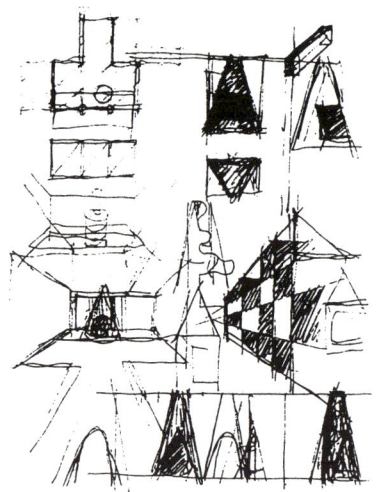

Andreas Fuhrimann & Gabrielle Hächler

Holiday house on the Rigi

Rigi, Scheidegg, Switzerland   *Photographs: Contributed by the architects*

The building has been situated in a peripheral position on the property, for the distance to the neighboring houses to be as large as possible and so that the option of constructing another building in the future would remain open.

The concrete cellar anchors the building into the sloping terrain and houses the entrance area and the technical and service rooms. Resting upon the stability of this plinth is the upper volume of the building, the footprint of which has a somewhat ship-like outline. This floor (ground floor on the side facing the slope) juts out eastward to a sufficient degree for a sheltered, protected, access area to be available, underneath the eaves.

The concrete chimney of the open fireplace rises like a mast out of the cellar and, together with a concrete wall, forms the bracing backbone behind which the two single-flight staircases connect the three floors. On the ground floor is a large living room spread over two different levels and with different ceiling heights. The deliberately low area in which the kitchen is contained creates a spatial feeling reminiscent of the sensation generated in the low parlors of the mountain cabins typical of local vernacular architecture. The 5-meter long fixed panorama window that frames the breathtaking view, perhaps the location's main asset, introduces a contemporary feeling of modernity. The polygonal floorplan allows the space to be divided into areas of subtly unusual proportions, which enhance the characteristics of the building and contribute to a refreshing perception of novelty within the timeless and spectacular scenery of the Alps. Moreover, the open fireplace is granted a suitably predominant position, at the widest spot in the room.

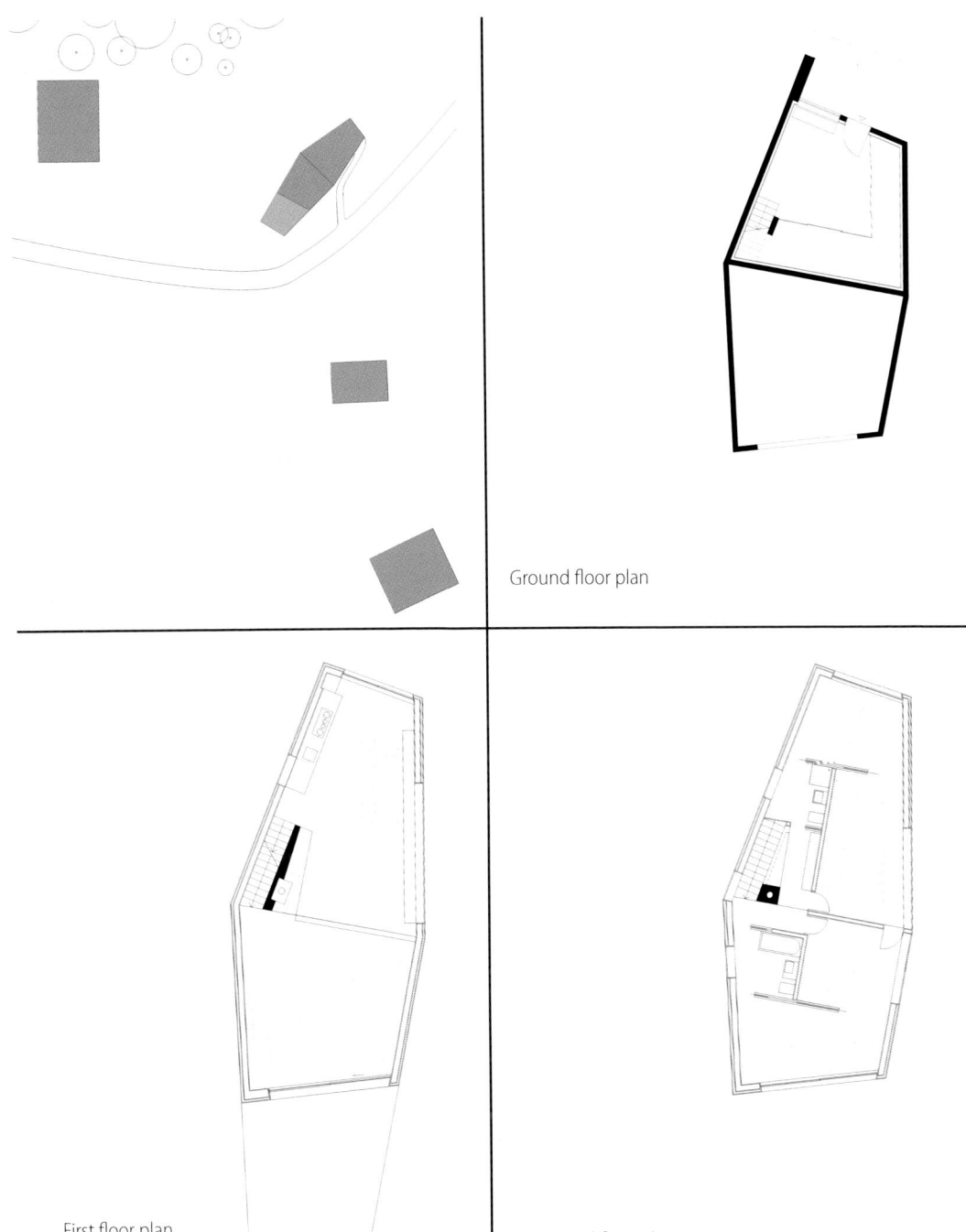

Ground floor plan

First floor plan

Second floor plan

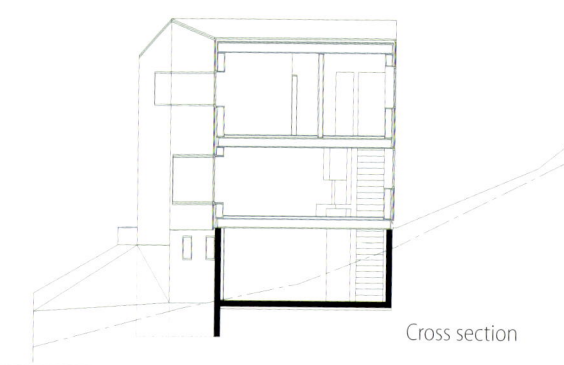

Cross section

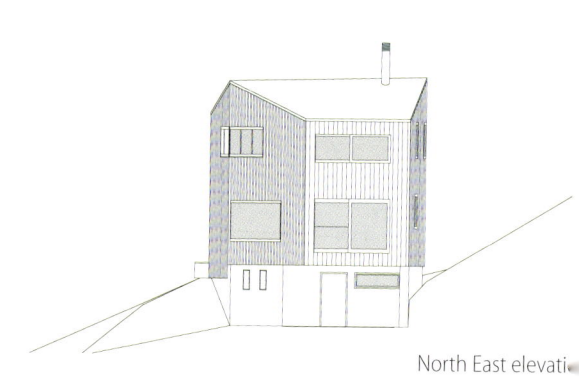

North East elevati

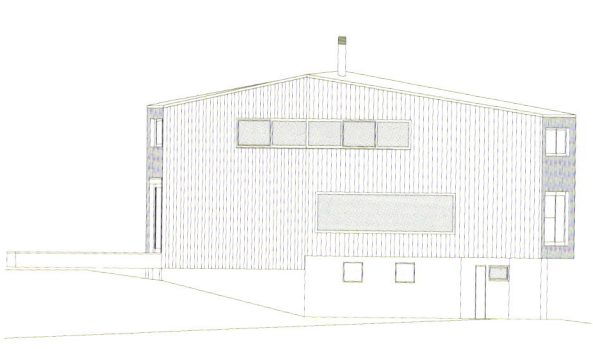

South East eleva

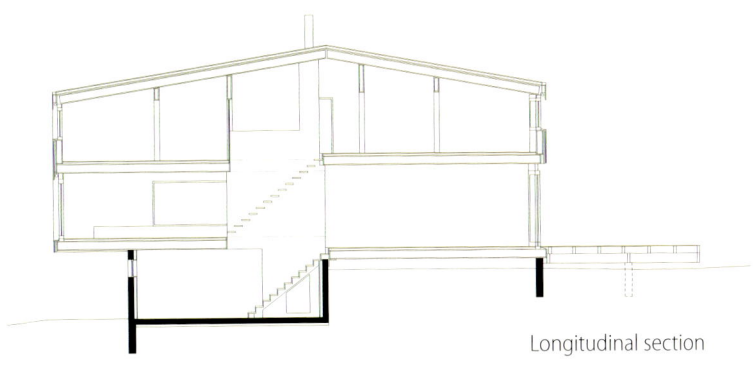

Longitudinal section

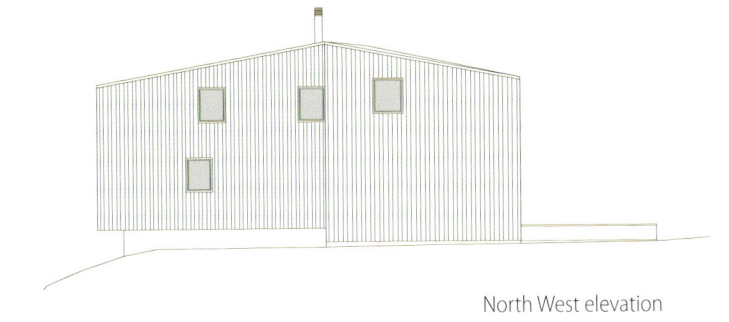

North West elevation

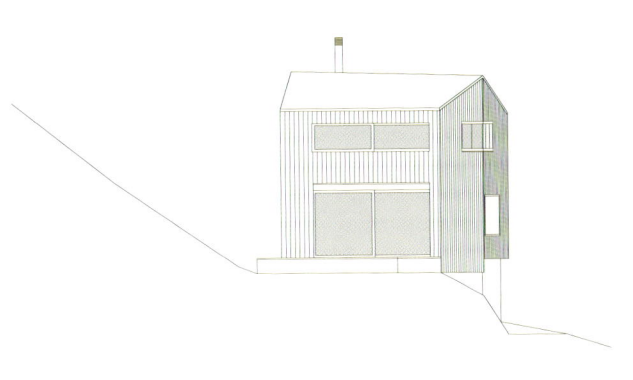

South West elevation

Blauraum Architekten

Salon Blauraum

HAMBURG, GERMANY *Photographs: Jörg Hempel, Blauraum Architekten*

Contemporary architecture and its concerns seem very foreign in Hamburg, a city of traders where the solid language of quick return is readily understood and respected. Corporate architectural firms control most of the market, and the numerous independent architects, less economically heavy-handed, are invited to sell their souls for the scraps.

When Rüdiger Ebel, Volker Halbach, Maurice Paulussen and Carsten Venus decided to start their practice here, they became aware it wasn't enough to find office space and go for it. One would have to create office space in a broader sense: a space of discourse and discussion from which a genuine architectural scene could emerge. So the four young architects started their office, Blauraum Architekten, and at the same time Salon Blauraum, as a forum specialized in design. More than a Café or a Gallery, the object is to maintain communication.

Both premises have separate entrances. Of the three street windows, the Salon has two. The first impression is of a closed cube, which then reveals its capacity to unfold by means of a series of hinged screens. One section displays a snack bar inside it, with a concealed kitchen work surface and a beautiful expresso machine. Another sector swivels around a central pivot, opening the way to a long corridor leading to various office spaces (conference room, plotter space).

The walls are faced with cork, to which office documents and notes can be pinned, as well as exhibits from the Salon. Office staff and Salon visitors mingle in the corridor, producing a creatively-stimulating overlap of work and play. In fact everything in the office is movable and can make room for larger public events or lectures.

The Salon provides an uncramped yet appropriate scenario for Blauraum architects to meet their clients. The unconventional work context is underlined by atmospheric lighting and glowing Formica desktops, bright textile hangings and comfortable chairs, a contemporary living room.

In the Salon the vertical boxes not only serve as espresso tables but as gallery pedestals. Thus the white cube gallery cliché is drawn towards the cocktail lounge ambience, and the cork wall tempts the public to become part of the show.

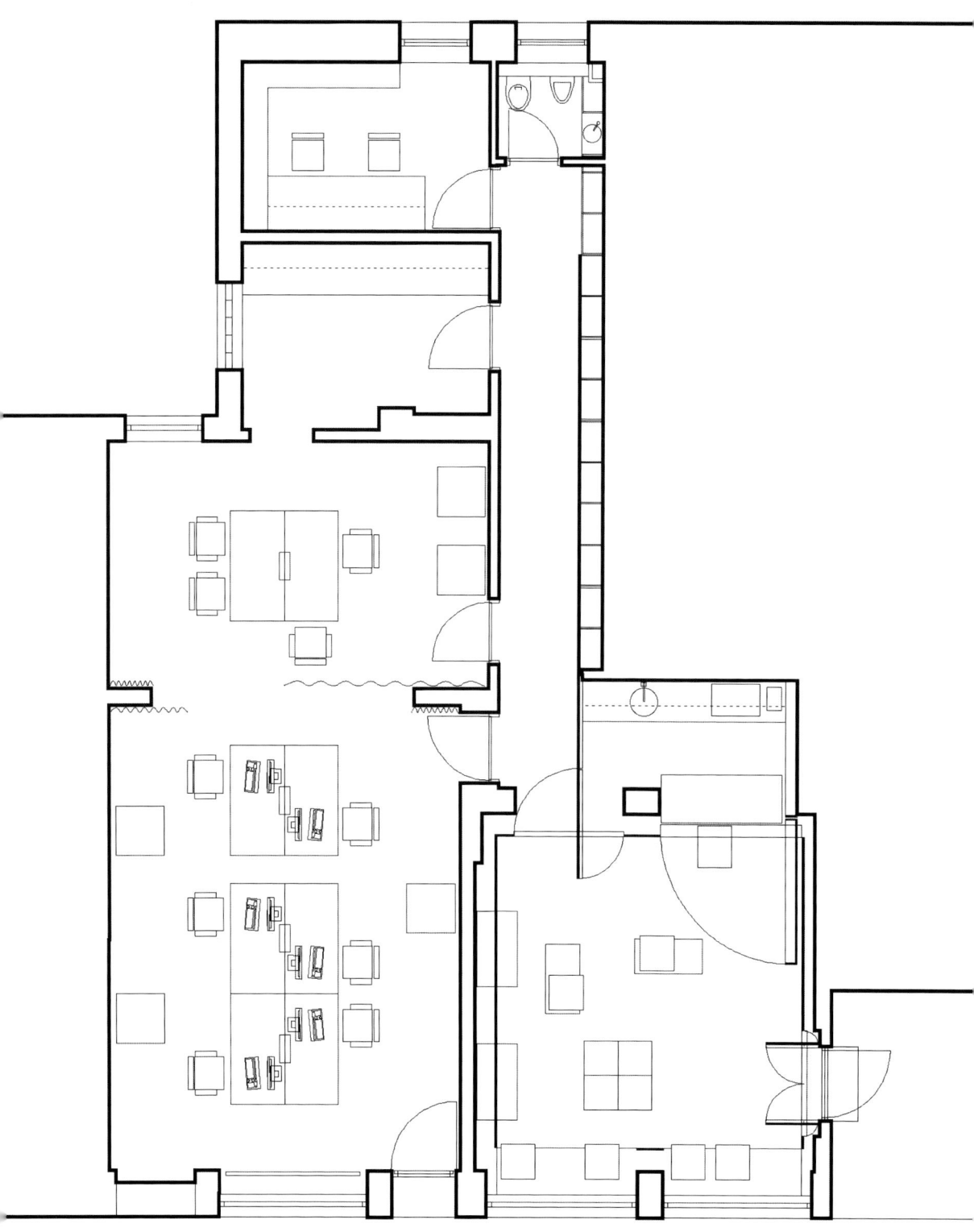

The four young architects started their office, Blauraum Architekten, and at the same time Salon Blauraum, as a forum specialized in design. To ensure a prominent profile they secured the premises on a busy street in the city center, a former shop with large display windows. One part of the shop took their offices. In the other a café with a design-oriented exhibition space was opened to attract the public and prompt conversation.

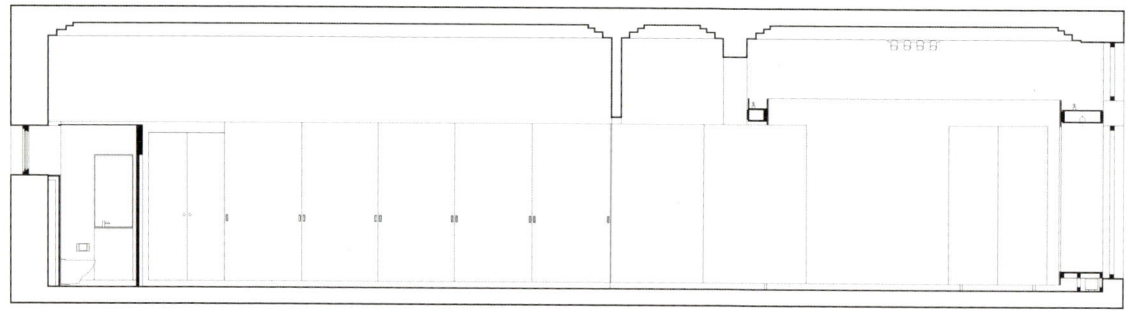

Section through corridor

The first impression is of a closed cube, which then reveals its capacity to unfold by means of a series of hinged screens. One section displays a snack bar inside it, with a concealed kitchen work surface and a beautiful espresso machine. Another sector swivels around a central pivot, opening the way to a long corridor leading to various office spaces (conference room, plotter space). The walls are faced with cork, to which office documents and notes can be pinned, as well as exhibits from the Salon.

Thomas Hanrahan & Victoria Meyers

Holley Loft

NEW YORK, USA *Photographs: Peter Aaron / Esto*

This project is an adaptation of an existing 4000 ft2 industrial loft space into a residence. The space is on the second floor of a loft building in lower Manhattan. In the final design, no solid walls were left. A single full-height wall of glass and steel marked the major division of master bedroom and bathroom from the rest of the apartment. From any position, the intention is to experience the full dimension of the entire loft space, with all the elements of the program distributed freely in the form of low cabinetry and movable panels. This disposition yields a complex space of constantly changing perspectives and points of view. Light from the short ends of the apartment penetrates deep into the residence, while the movable panels allow for the creation of smaller, more intimate spaces to accommodate overnight guests.

The major division within the space is made by a 48ft long raw steel and glass wall. This marks the division between the master bedroom/master bath area and the rest of the apartment with sandblasted areas for privacy. The area covered by the curtain is clear glass. The movement of the curtain allows the inhabitant of the space to control its openness.

Opposite the steel and glass wall is a 30ft long maple cabinet, which contains an objectified fragment of the steel and glass wall plane. Here, in order to mark its displacement, the wall curves. This cabinet also marks a boundary between the living spaces and a kitchen/guest bath. Translucent materials hang through a wood cabinet at specific locations to partially reveal the space beyond.

Full-height painted wood panels can either close down the rear of the apartment or remain in a fully open position. When they are open the panels float in the space: closed they demarcate one room; closed further, two rooms. The disposition of these spaces changes throughout the day according to the inhabitants' requirements.

Floor plan
1. Entrance
2. Living Room
3. Gallery
4. Dining Room
5. Kitchen
6. Master bedroom
7. Guest bedroom

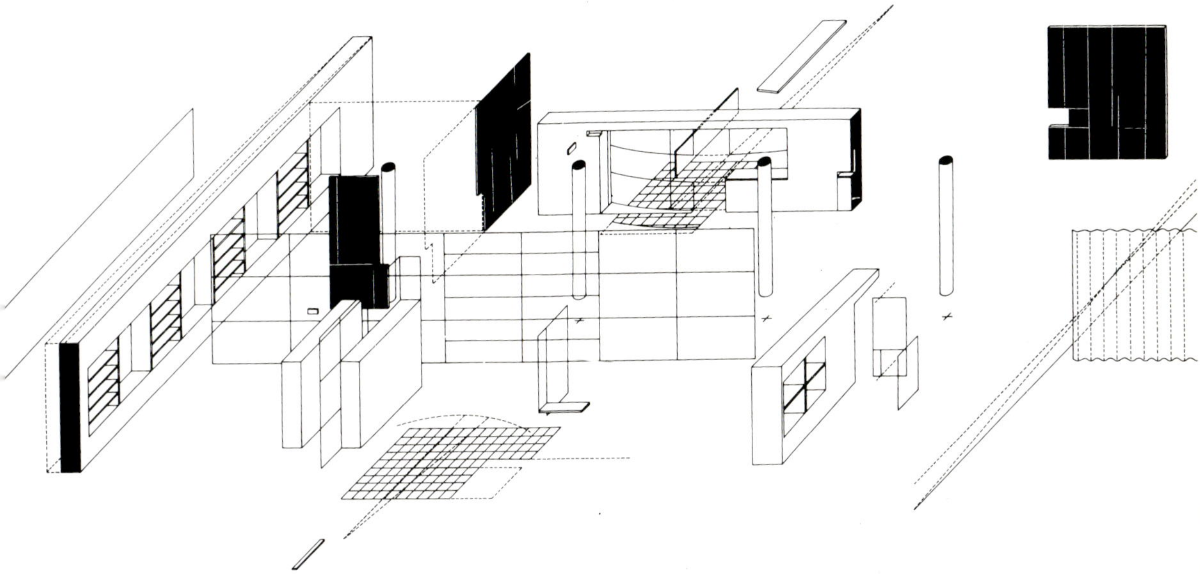

167

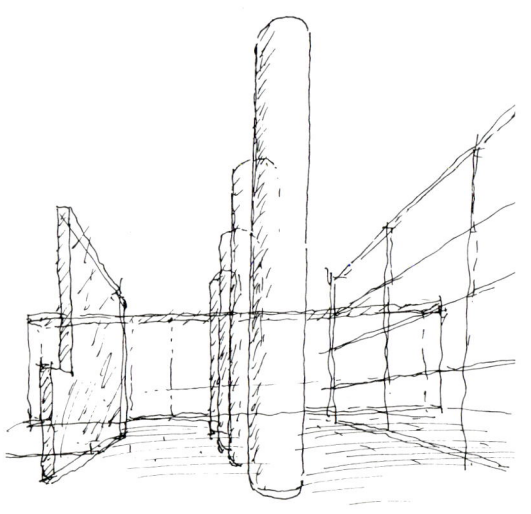

Full-height painted wood panels can either close down the rear of the apartment or remain in a fully open position. When they are open the panels float in the space: closed they demarcate one room; closed further, two rooms.

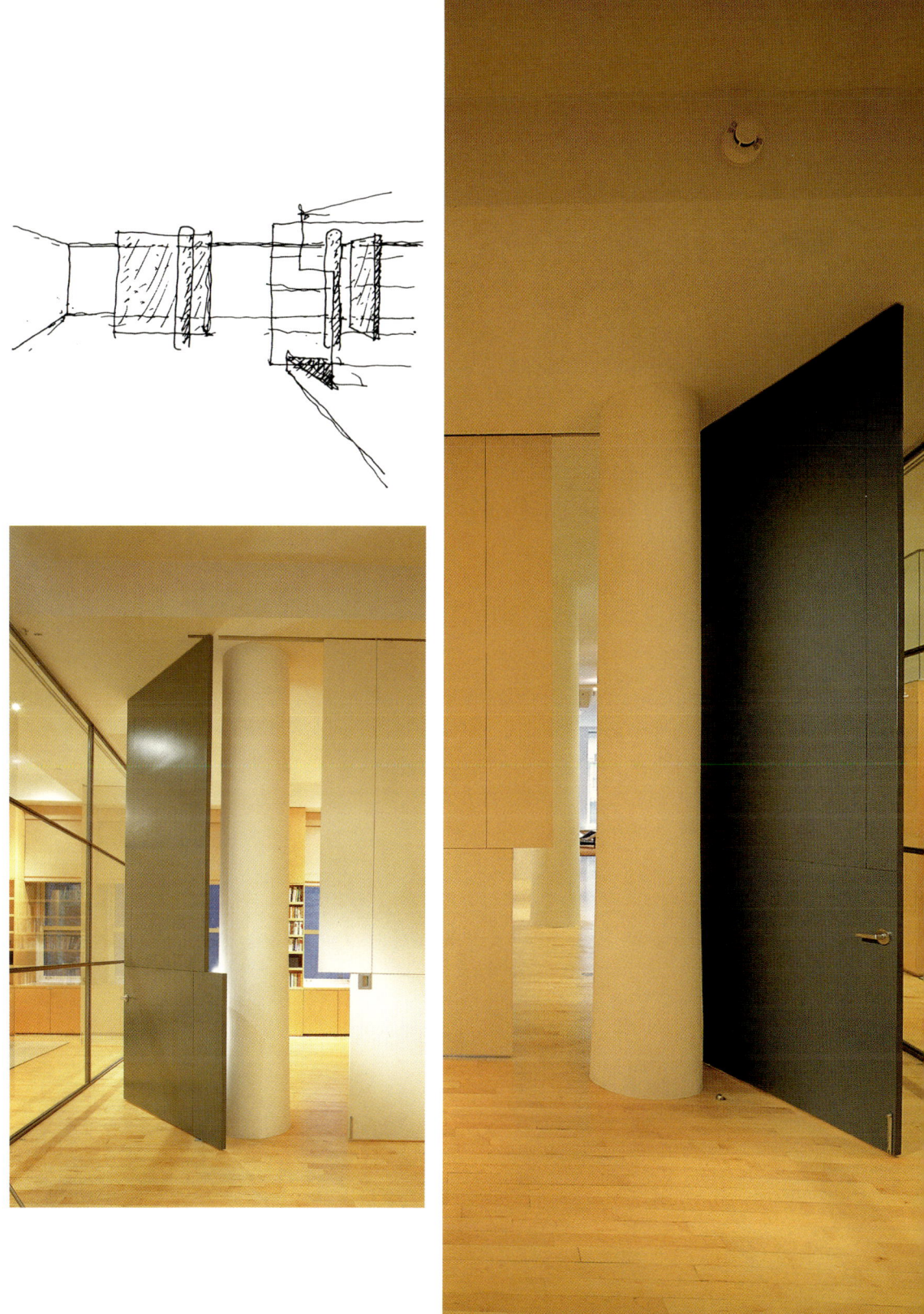

Eva Prats y Ricardo Flores

A house in a suitcase

BARCELONA, SPAIN   *Photographs: Eugeni Pons*

The concept was carried out in an attic of Barcelona's Ensanche district. The rectangular space is 3 m wide and high, by 9 m long. There is a small space on the side with the sanitary installation, which doesn't regard the present considerations. The only opening outdoors is the skylight that runs down the full length of the room. It is a temporary dwelling, used by people who travel a lot with little luggage. The apartment only contains the zenithal light that floods it and two large closed volumes. These pieces of furniture have been designed like the trunks of the great travelers, the content dictating the container (let's remember the compact traveling wardrobes and writing desks invented by Louis Vuitton, which opened up to become pieces of furniture with all a person's needs). The reduced space doesn't permit objects to accumulate and one of the guidelines of the design was to prevent dust from gathering during the periods when it is empty.

The project researches the minimum occupation our activities require; the trunks open their various facets revealing unguessed uses which divide the space into fragments at a human scale, for precise chores. The free space varies in form and function throughout the day. The larger body contains the largest object, the bed, and also the smallest: a sliding shelf to place jewelry or pills. The doors of the dormitory trunk act as a screen to conceal dressing or undressing. It also has a luggage rack, a mirror and two bedside tables with reading lamps and a drawer for the bedclothes. The bed slides away under the hall landing and the bed head can double as a sofa back. Out of the kitchen trunk slide shelves and tables. An upper shelf hides the kitchen from the entrance hall. A breakfast table slides out next to the china cupboard and the larder.

Before leaving everything is hidden again.

Until the next visit the door closes on a room full of light and two giant traveling trunks.

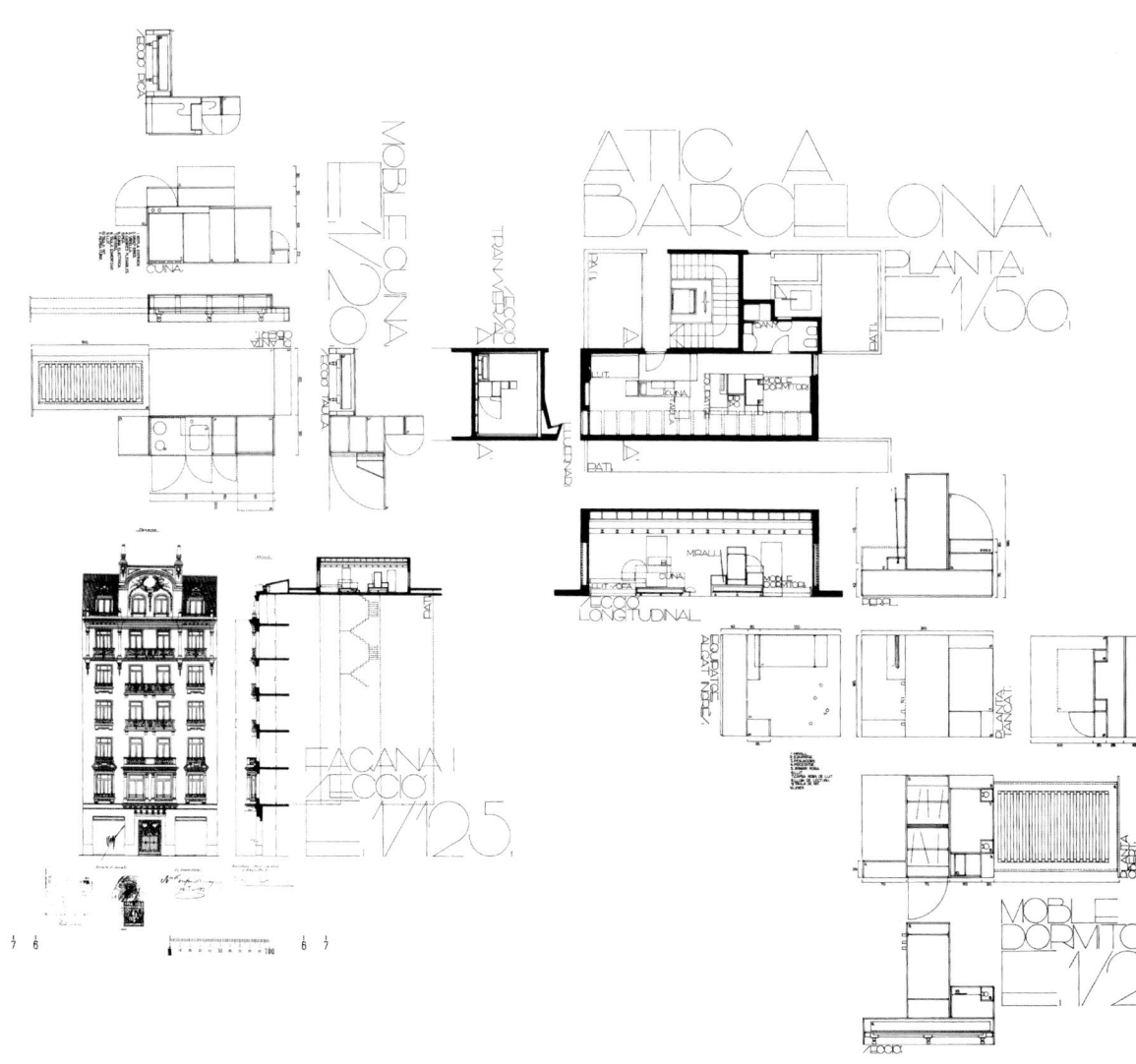

Dimensions of the space: 9x3x3.
Dimensions of the dormitory trunk: 2,10m x 1,60m x 1,90m high.
Dimensions of the kitchen trunk: 2,00m x 1,65m x 1,20m high.

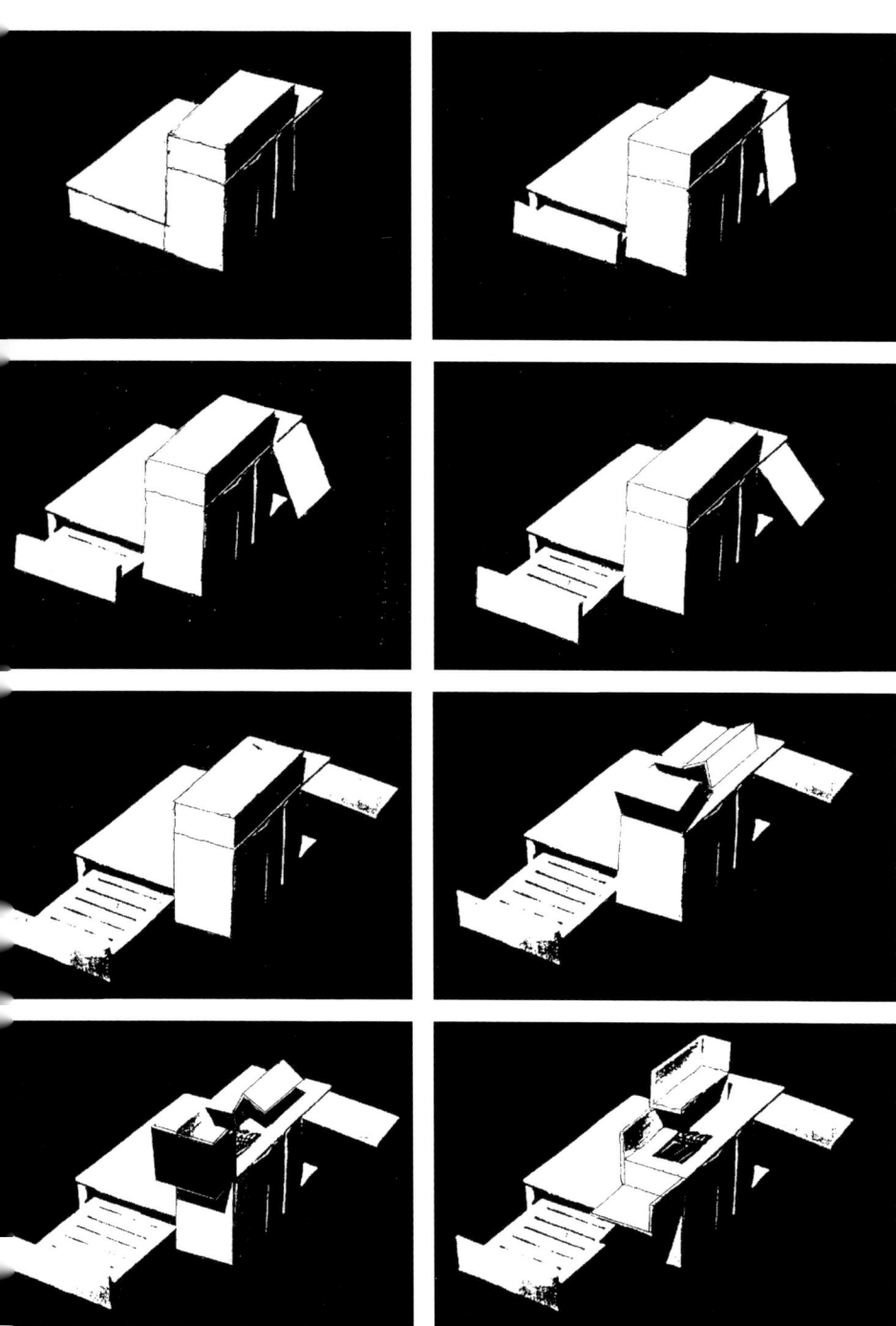

Before leaving everything is hidden again. Until the next visit the door closes on a room full of light and two giant traveling trunks.

JAHN Associates

Kutti Beach House

VAUCLUSE, AUSTRALIA *Photographs: John Gollings*

Recently moved to Australia from England, the clients commissioned the design and construction of their new family home. It was designed to enhance the quality of life of its occupants, paying particular attention to the amenities of the surroundings, the idea being to establish distinctive ties between the building and streetscape, and between the building and harbor.

On a conceptual level, the project avoids the usual typology of a single mass in the center of the site with minimal setbacks to side boundaries. Instead, the plan is split, with a timber-framed harbor pavilion on the north and a load-bearing masonry street-side wing on the south, creating a courtyard in the center of the program. This provides greater capacity for ventilation, natural light and views to all the rooms from multiple perspectives.

Each component has its own individual architectonic character, while at the same time sitting in harmony with the other aspects of the program. The harbor (summer) pavilion is designed to capture the atmosphere of a beach house, while the stone-clad street (winter) wing provides enclosure and warmth and is more urban. The design creates a choice of internal and external living areas that are responsive to climate and that maximize access to harbor views, sunlight and ventilation. In planning terms, it is a model solution for large sites.

The rich palette of materials creates an organic interplay of textures and tones. The exterior walls are clad in Western red cedar weatherboards, the warmth of which perfectly complements the colder tones of the rendered masonry and split face Mintaro slate placed at seemingly random heights and thicknesses. Inside, Western red cedar weatherboards also line the walls as well as rendered and set plaster masonry. The floor finishes consist of recycled blackbutt from Queensland, 600X600mm lineal-cut travertine with off-white sand/cement slurry fill and Vietnamese bluestone, the latter gracing the entry level. In concert with the wall cladding, both inside and out, the window and door frames are also in Western red cedar, except for those with 'frameless' glazing.

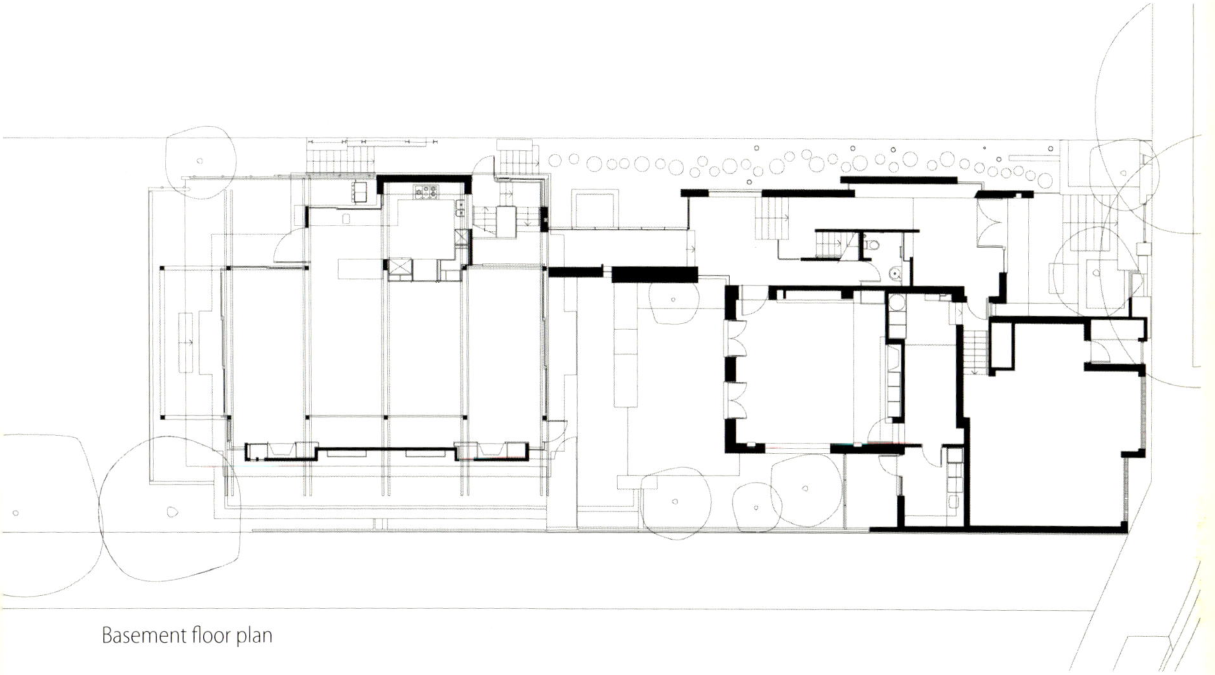

Basement floor plan

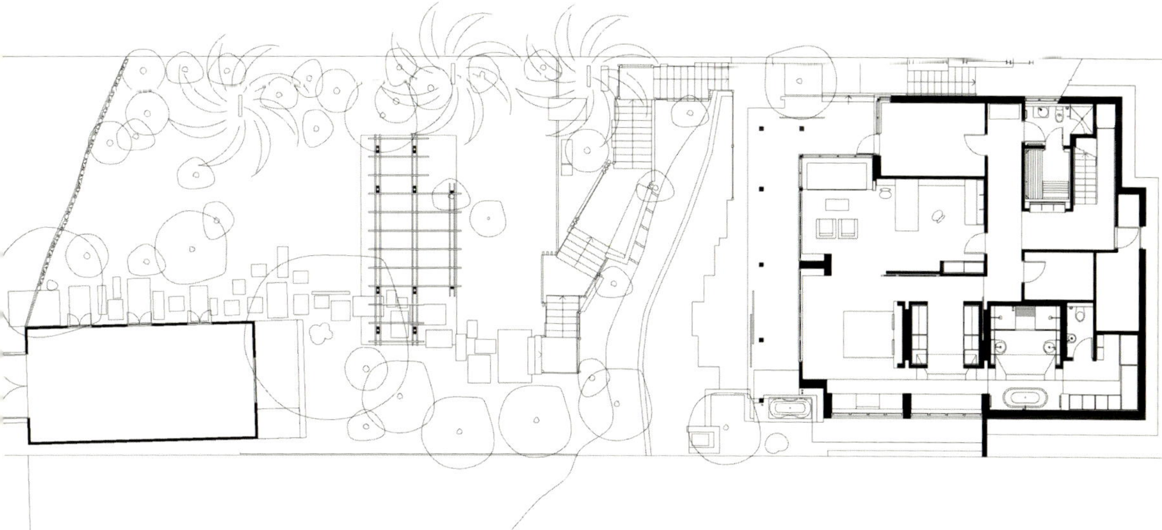

Ground floor plan

191

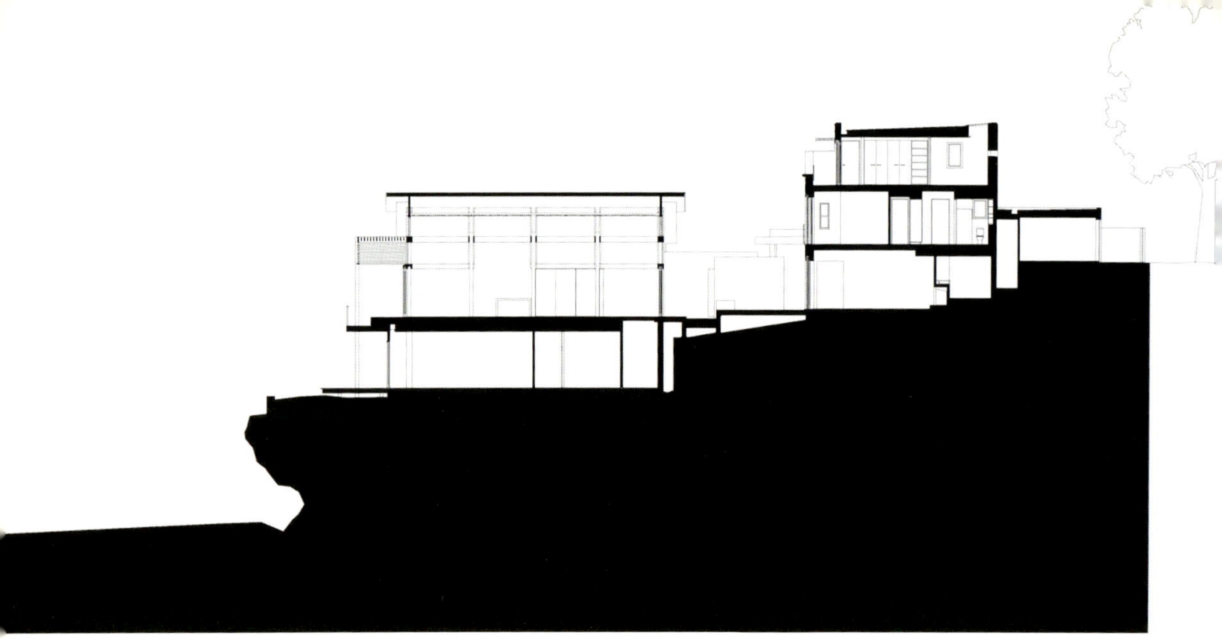

Longitudinal section

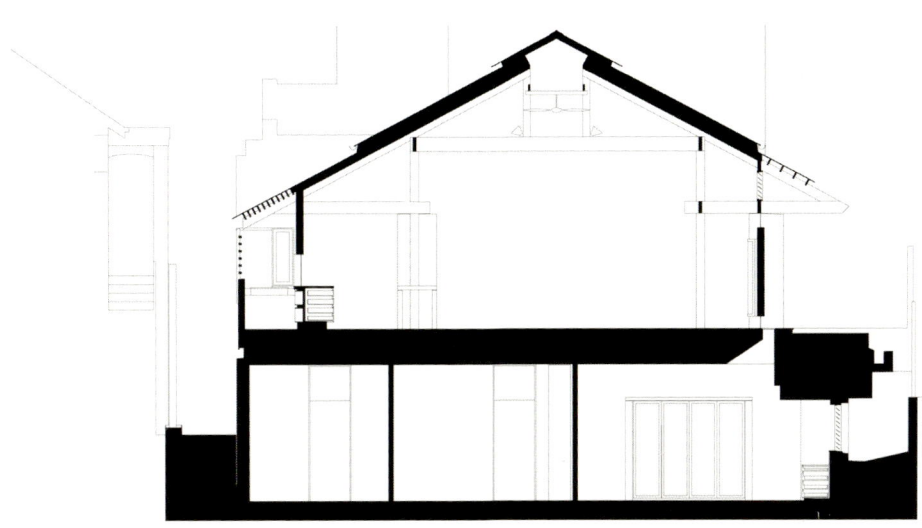
Cross section

Felipe Assadi

Buzeta House

Maitencillo, Puchuncaví, Chile

Photographs: Guy Wenborne

Buzeta house is a single-family summer house located to the south of Maitencillo, standing on a terrain of 1800 sqm (19,400 sqft) and perched at the top of a steep slope, 120 meters (390 feet) above the sea. Conditions in the area are excellent for paragliding, which is why the volume has been positioned to face the wind, strengthening the presence of the slope and generating spectacular views over the sea.

The volume appears from the east as an entirely opaque façade composed of a double skin of small boards, which conceals the views on arrival. The lateral façades contain two round windows, which, together with the steep slope on the western flank and the sea in the background, conjure up the image of a ship. The main façade leans toward the ocean revealing stunning panoramic views through a huge window, which allows the changing natural light to penetrate to the interior, throughout the course of the day. At night the roles are reversed and the interior lighting casts a soft light on the boards of the back wall, reflecting the warmth of the materials and of the house itself.

Despite the bizarre cross-section, the 112 sqm (1,200 sqft) floor plan, is perfectly rectangular and the interior is laid out symmetrically, ordered by a double-height space to which the rooms of the house are attached. A curved roof, lined with copper, inspired by the wind-swollen sails of the paragliders, runs uniformly across the house from east to west, becoming a weft of wooden boards and providing shade for the sea-facing rooms.

The materials used are Radiata pine for the structure, Oregon pine for the exterior and copper for the roofs and chimneys.

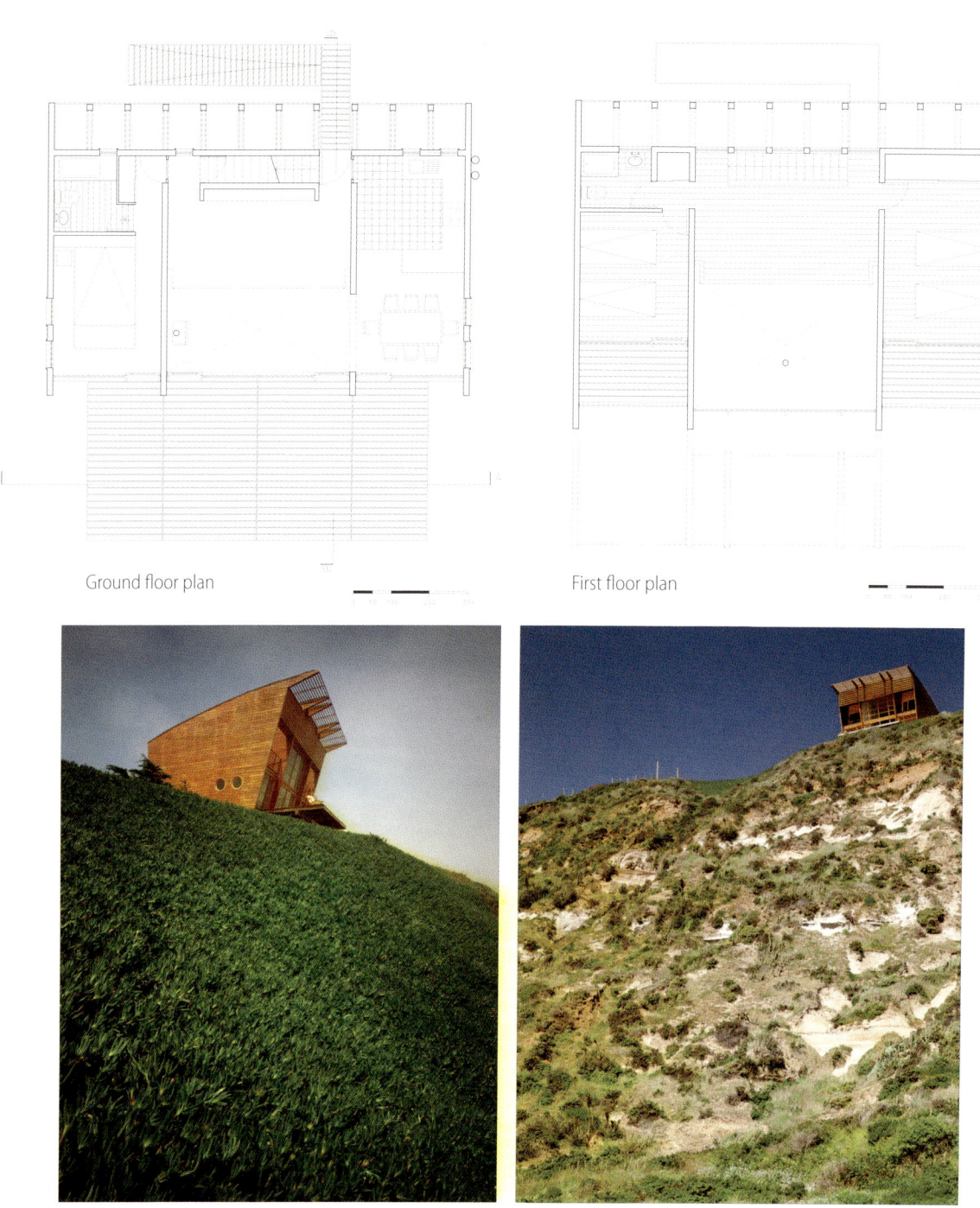

Ground floor plan

First floor plan

East elevation

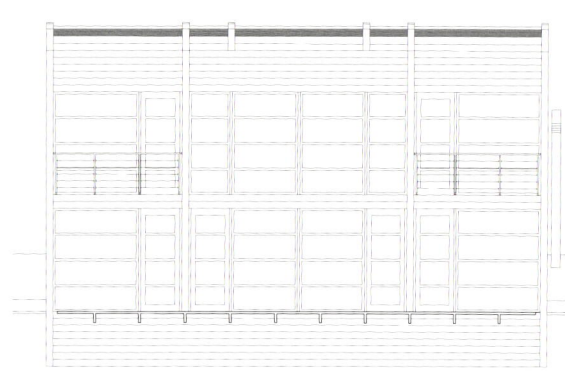
Section A

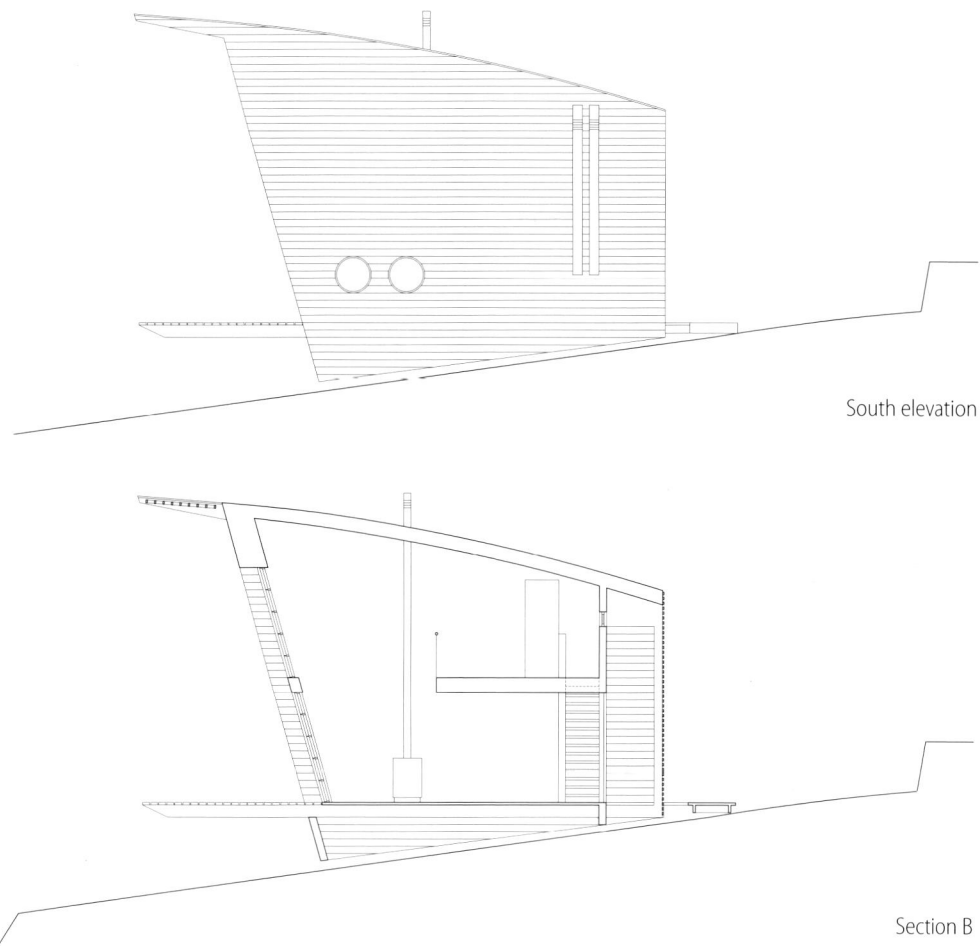

South elevation

Section B

The main façade leans toward the ocean revealing stunning panoramic views through a huge window, which allows the changing natural light to penetrate to the interior, throughout the course of the day.

Peter Hulting Architect

Guest Appearance

GOTHENBURG, SWEDEN *Photographs: James Silverman*

When Swedish architect Peter Hulting was asked to transform this old farm site into a couple's new home, he immediately saw the potential to create an unpretentious, sensitive space with the ability to connect both to its immediate surroundings and the neighboring open landscape. Specific only in their demands for a concrete floor and clay roof tiles, quality craftsmanship and simplicity were key to the couple's vision of "a house that could age with dignity".

Walking into this small summer house situated on Sweden's west coast peninsula, you are immediately struck by a sense of space that belies its 538 square feet (50 sq m) of floor space. Everything from the furniture to the lighting has been designed to enhance the building's shape and size - from the elongated Japanese-style table and benches, to the long steel-pipe chimney that guides the eye upwards from the open fire to the wooden ceiling.

A combination of wood, concrete and plaster creates a range of tactile surfaces that compare and contrast in equal measure. The smooth concrete floor incorporates the water-carried heating system, while the use of sawed larch tree for the exterior walls and reclaimed clay tiles on the roof allow the building to sit perfectly within this picturesque setting.

In order to maximize on the available space, Hulting opted for an open plan design. By creating a large glass frontage overlooking the south-facing landscape, sliding doors define the inner space when required, while at the same time ensuring the interior of the guesthouse remains cool in the summer.

Creating compact solutions in such a reduced space was central to the design concept; this was achieved, in part, by allowing the dividing walls to work like large pieces of furniture within the main space. Towards one end a wardrobe doubles as a wall divider, separating the sleeping area from the rest of the house. The reverse of this wardrobe doubles as a set of bookshelves at the foot of the bed. There is also space for two loft beds here, while the simple design of Ulf Scherlin's "Birå 4" cupboard ensures that any clutter is neatly stored away out of sight.

To the left of the bedroom, two sliding doors conceal the toilet and shower areas. The floors, tiled in Portuguese stone, offset standard white tiles that have been 'brick-mounted' and finished with a dark grey grout.

The kitchen sits in a semi-recess, cleverly defining its parameters without encroaching on the open-plan design of the overall space. The stainless steel of the kitchen contrasts beautifully with brightly colored handmade Portuguese tiles.

The shape of the dining table and benches add to the sense of space. Large sliding glass doors capitalize on the view and provide easy access to the exterior deck.

Drexler Guinand Jauslin

Weekend House

Pigniu/Panix, Switzerland

Photographs: Ralph Feiner

The village Pigniu/Panix is situated at 1300 meters above sea level, in the Surselva region of Graubünden, above Ilanz. The house is situated above the centre of the village. Although it is clearly a house of our time it is well integrated in the village's general appearance.

The building consists of two main floors, surmounted by a completely open third floor, merely enclosed by the two slopes of the gabled roof and by a sheer glass triangle at either end. A band surrounds the whole volume on its two main levels, concrete, for the plinth downstairs, wooden shingles for the upper living floor. The concrete band emerges from the landscape, to end at the street entrance to the house – from where the structure reads most clearly. A shift between the two levels articulates the volume's upper and lower halves, loosening the mass of the building and connecting it to the alpine environment. As fire regulations require a higher safety distance for wooden walls, the two upper floors stand partly shifted laterally off their concrete plinth.

The materials were chosen in accordance to the surrounding houses and barns. Its constructive language connects traditional and modern elements and techniques. The lower part is entirely of concrete with flat modular formwork – the upper part is of prefabricated wooden elements, clad with hand-cut larch shingles. The larch windows and shutters are the same for both parts – thereby accentuating the continuity of the band.

Despite its integrated exterior, the 150 sqm interior is distributed in a clearly contemporary manner, divided only by different levels and by sliding walls around the lower bedrooms. The continuity of the spiral is reflected in the spatial structure and determines the daily movement and flow of its inhabitants. The soapstone fireplace is the hinge of the movement, which continues throughout the three levels, from the stove to the "chaise très longue", to the kitchen.

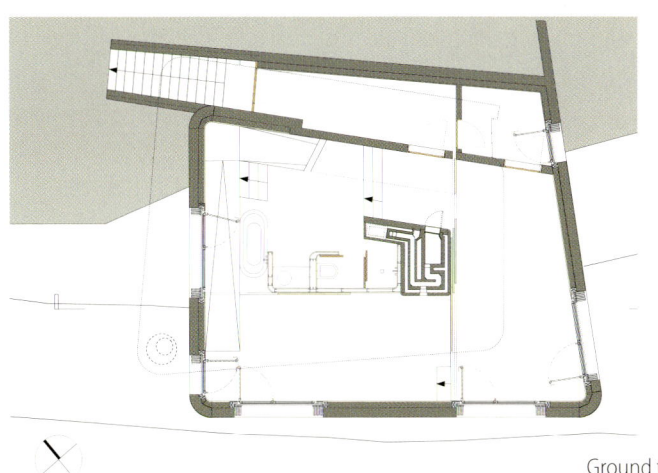

Ground floor plan

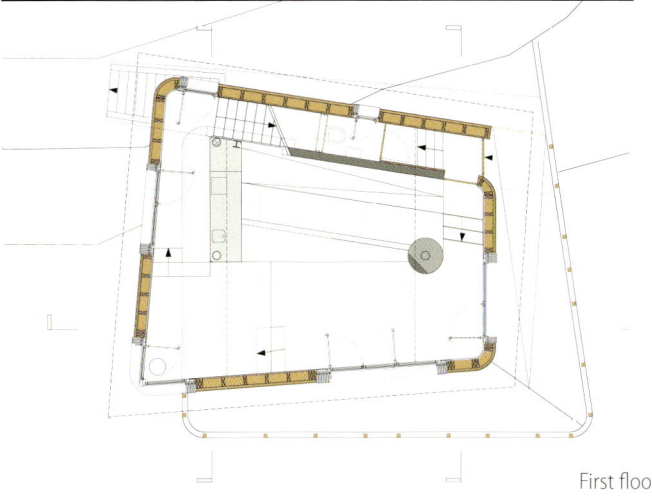

First floor plan

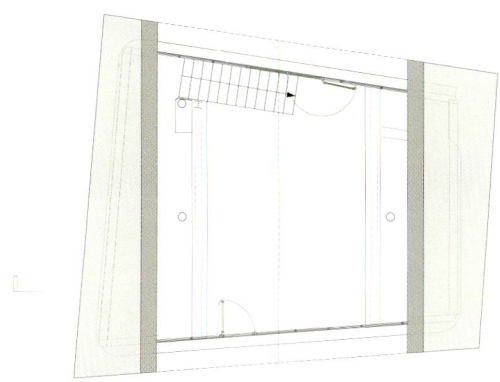

Attic plan

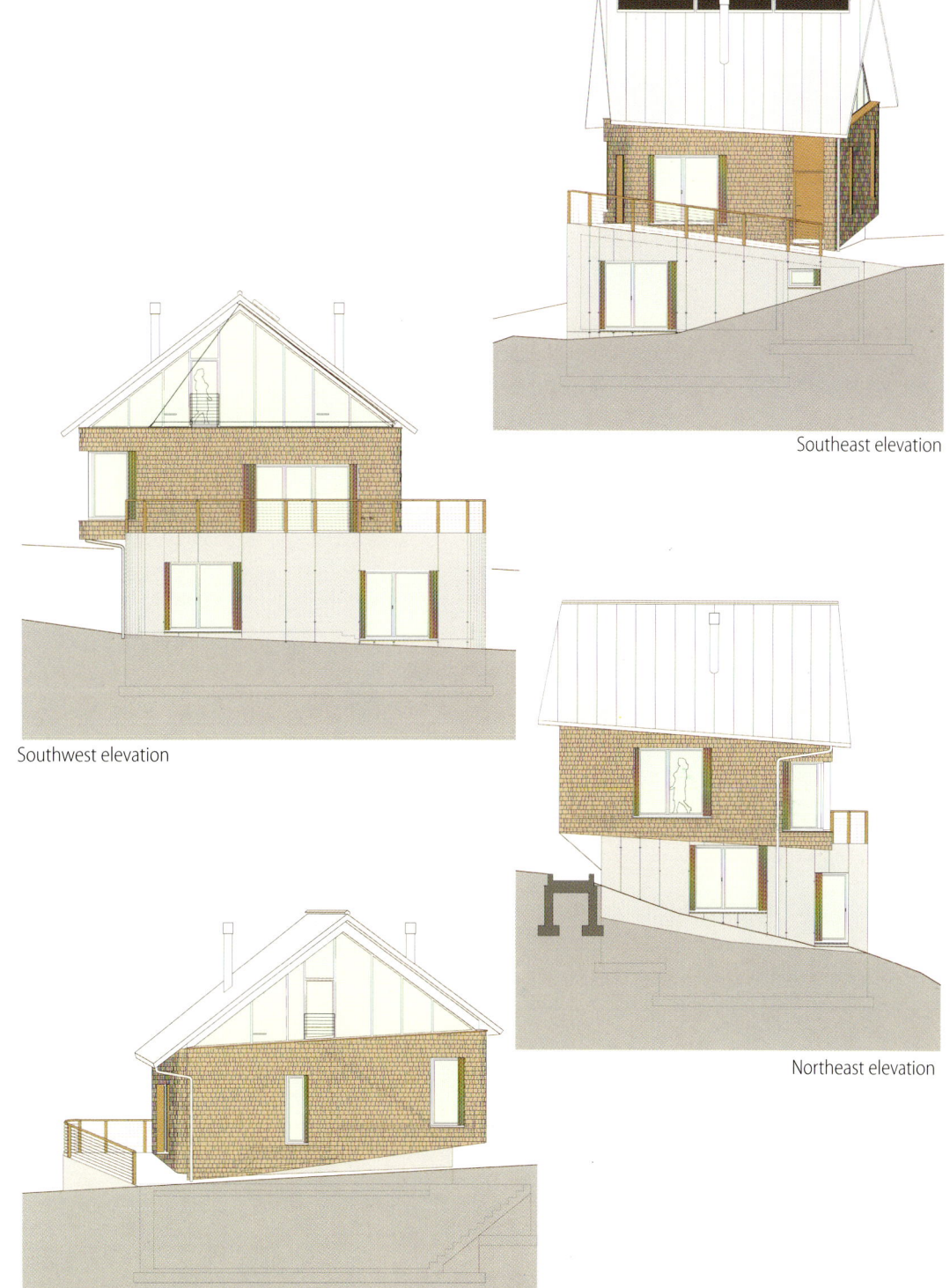

Southeast elevation

Southwest elevation

Northeast elevation

Northwest elevation

229

EDGE DESIGN INSTITUTE

Suitcase House

BEIJING, PEOPLE'S REPUBLIC OF CHINA *Photographs: Howard Chang, Gary Chang*

In 2000, SOHO China Ltd. invited 12 young architects from South Korea, Japan, Taiwan, Singapore, Thailand, Mainland China and Hong Kong, to design 11 houses and a clubhouse in the valley at the foot of the Great Wall.

Rethinking the proverbial image of a house, Suitcase House Hotel questions the nature of intimacy, privacy, spontaneity and flexibility, in pursuit of infinite adaptable scenarios, unfolding the mechanics of domestic (p)leisure.

The 2696.356 sqft (250.5 sqm) building, completed in October 2001 at the head of the Nangou Valley, is oriented to maximize views of the Great Wall and solar exposure in the temperate continental climate.

The base of the building's three strata is a concrete plinth, which contains the pantry, a servant's room, the boiler room and the sauna. The middle layer cantilevers outward from the concrete plinth that anchors the steel structure above. Everything is clad in the same timber, blurring boundaries between in and out, building and furniture. This level is for habitation, activity and flow. The layout is non-hierarchical; movable items of the shell adapt to the activity, number of occupants, or preferences regarding privacy. The open volume turns into a sequence of rooms, each singularized by a specific role. Concealed under a landscape of pneumatically assisted floor panels, several function-specific compartments may be "unfolded". Only what is in use is present at any one time. Besides the basic bedroom, bathroom, kitchen and storage, there is a meditation chamber (with glazed floor looking down the valley), music chamber, library, study, lounge, and a fully equipped sauna. If guests arrive in the evening, the entire space, 144 x161/2ft (44 x 5 m), can turn into a single lounge. If the party goes on late, seven guest rooms can be unfolded, accommodating up to 14 people.

The exterior is an envelope of full height double-glazed folding doors; the inner layer is a series of screens. The façade pattern is rooted in its user-oriented logic. The various entrances hold equal status and their use decides the distribution.

A pull-down ladder leads to the roof, the top stratum, with a 360° view.

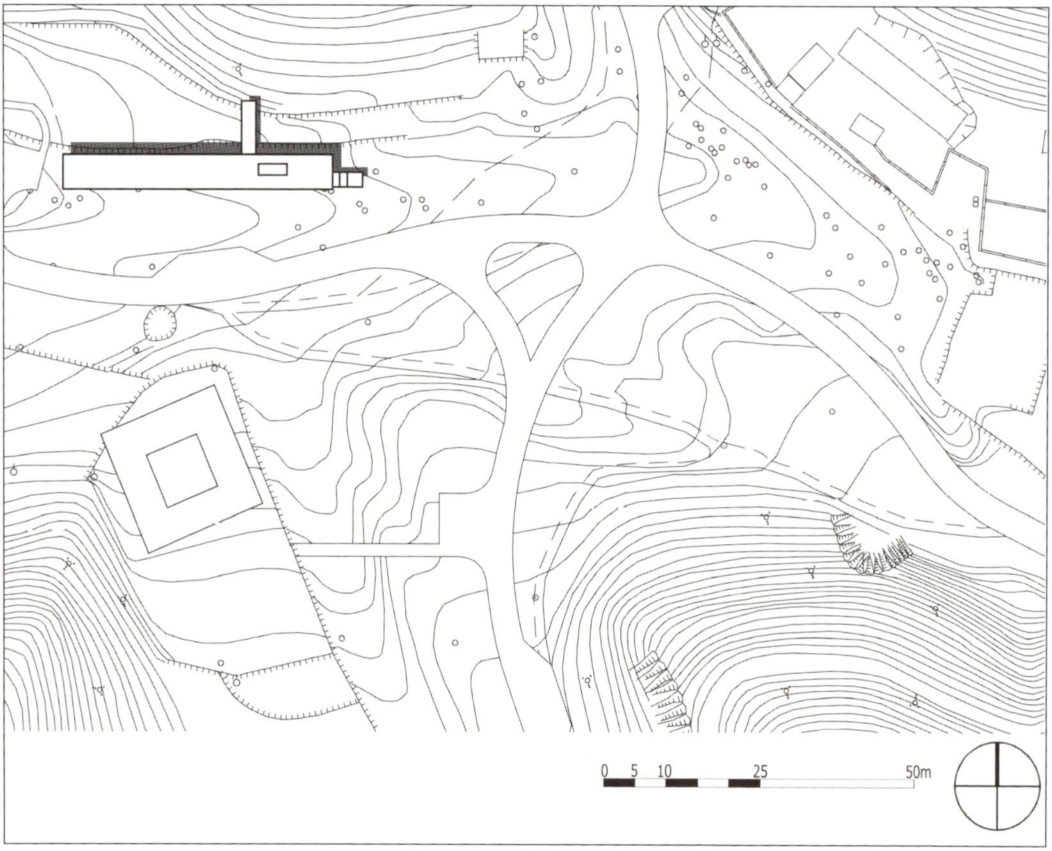

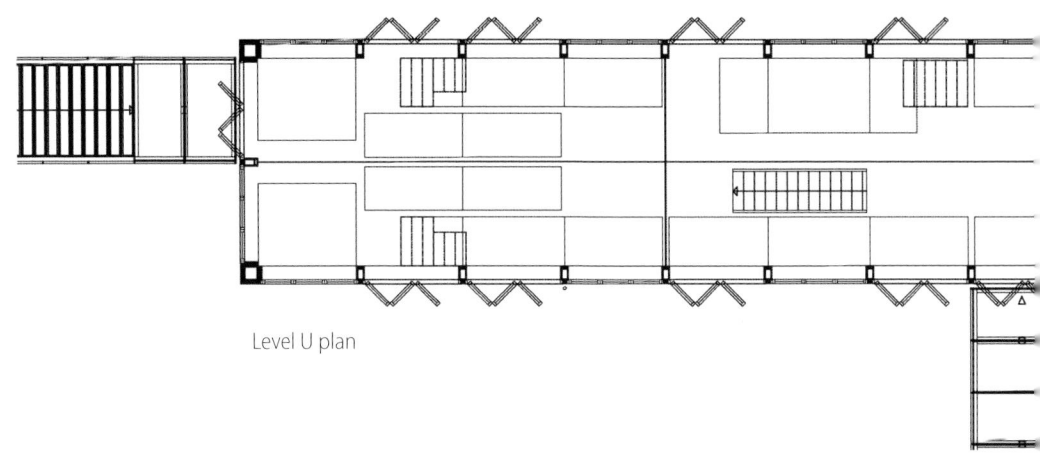

Level U plan

1. Living
2. Dining
3. Bedroom
4. Storage
5. Bathing
6. Study
7. Kitchen
8. Cloak room
9. Meditation
10. Audio/visual
11. Library
12. Sauna
13. Laundry
14. Pantry
15. Boiler room
16. Butler's bedroom
17. Butler's bathroom

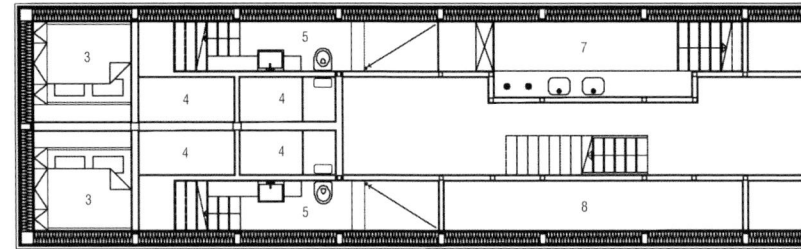

Level M plan

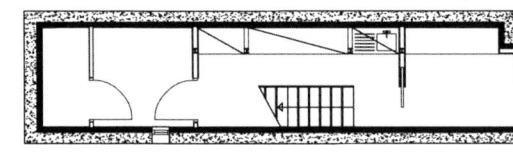

Level L plan

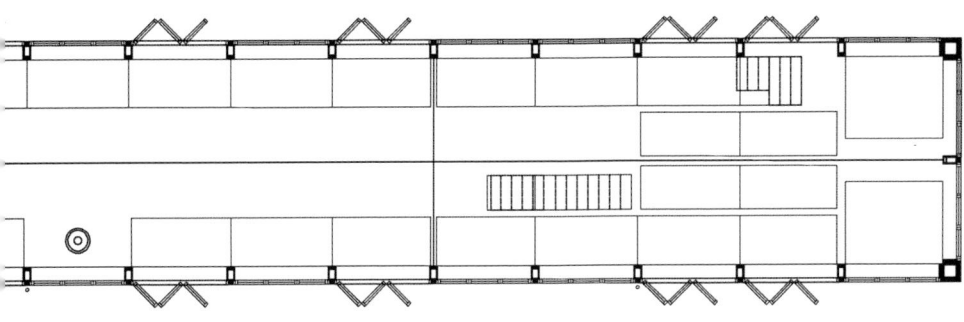

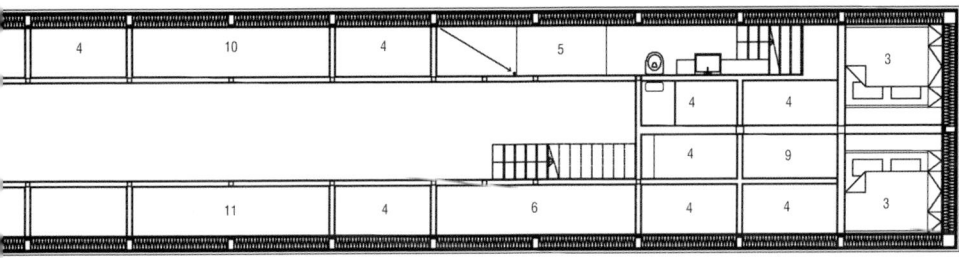

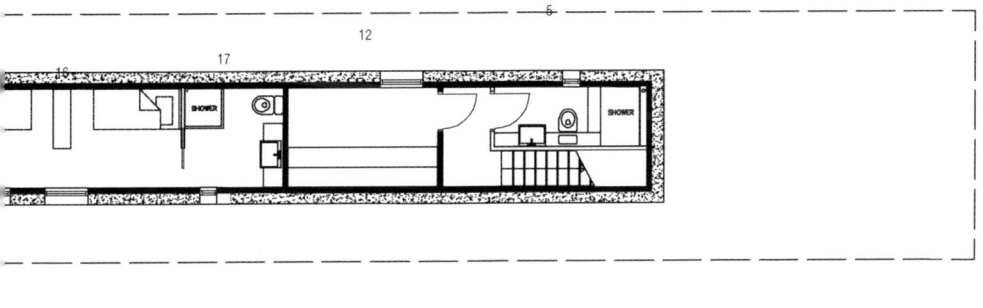

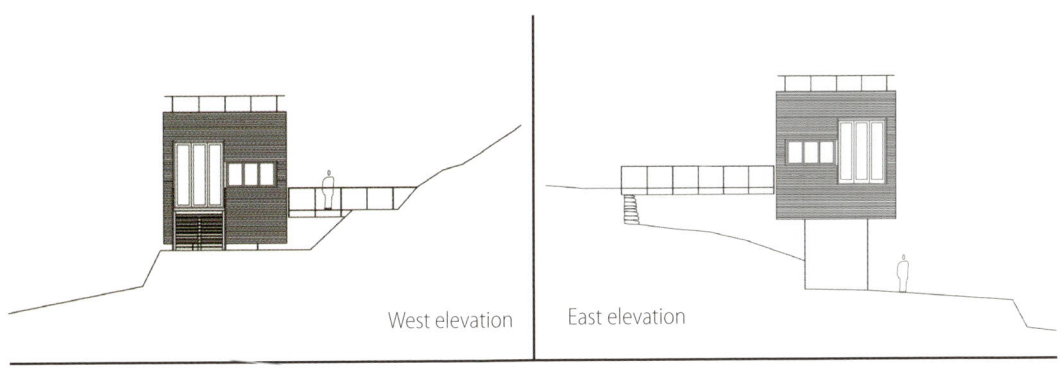

West elevation   East elevation

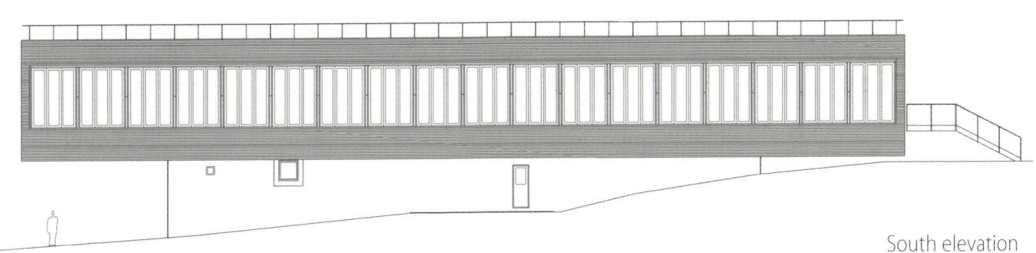

South elevation

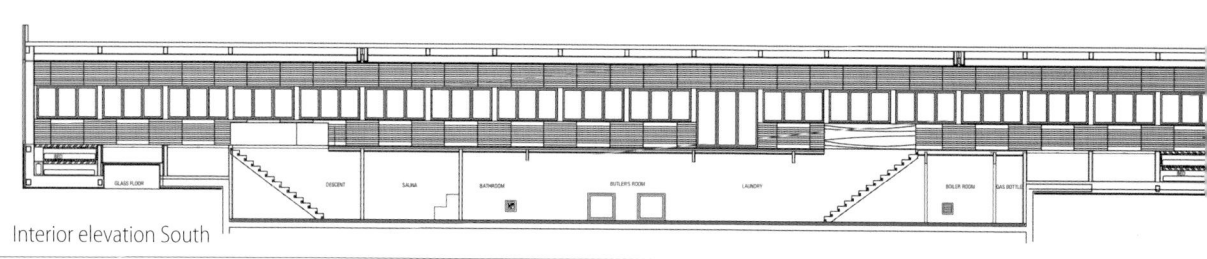

Interior elevation South

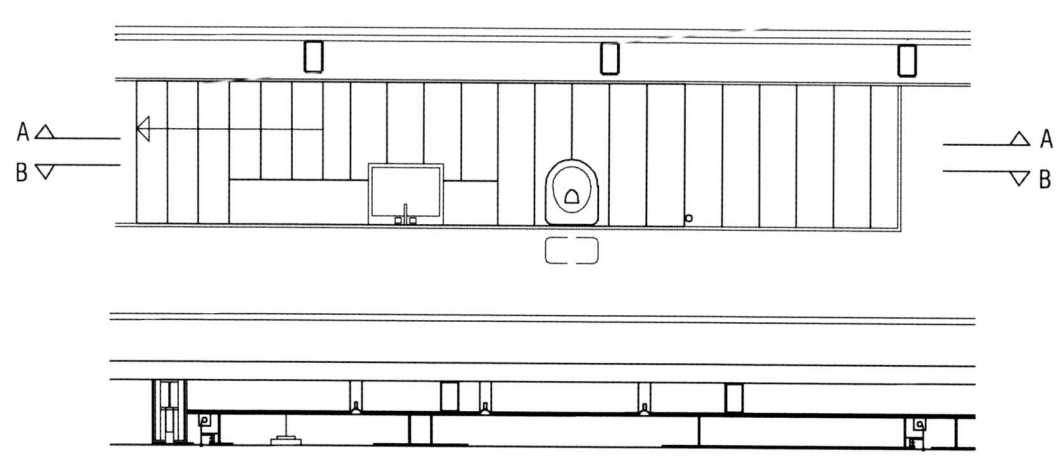

Bathroom

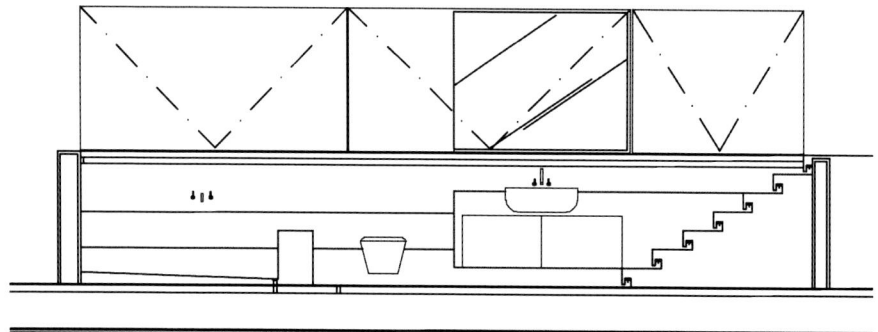

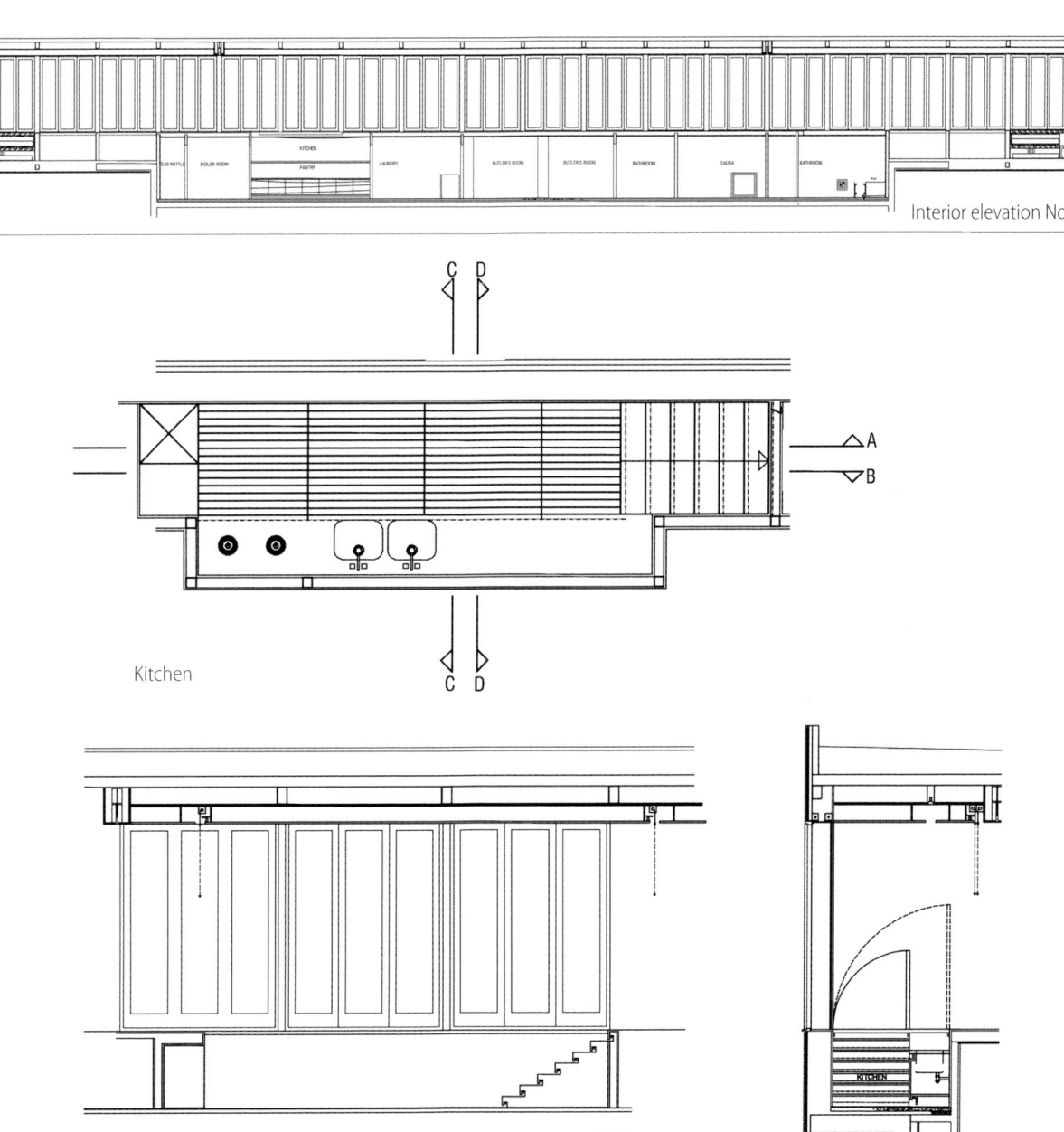

Interior elevation North

Kitchen

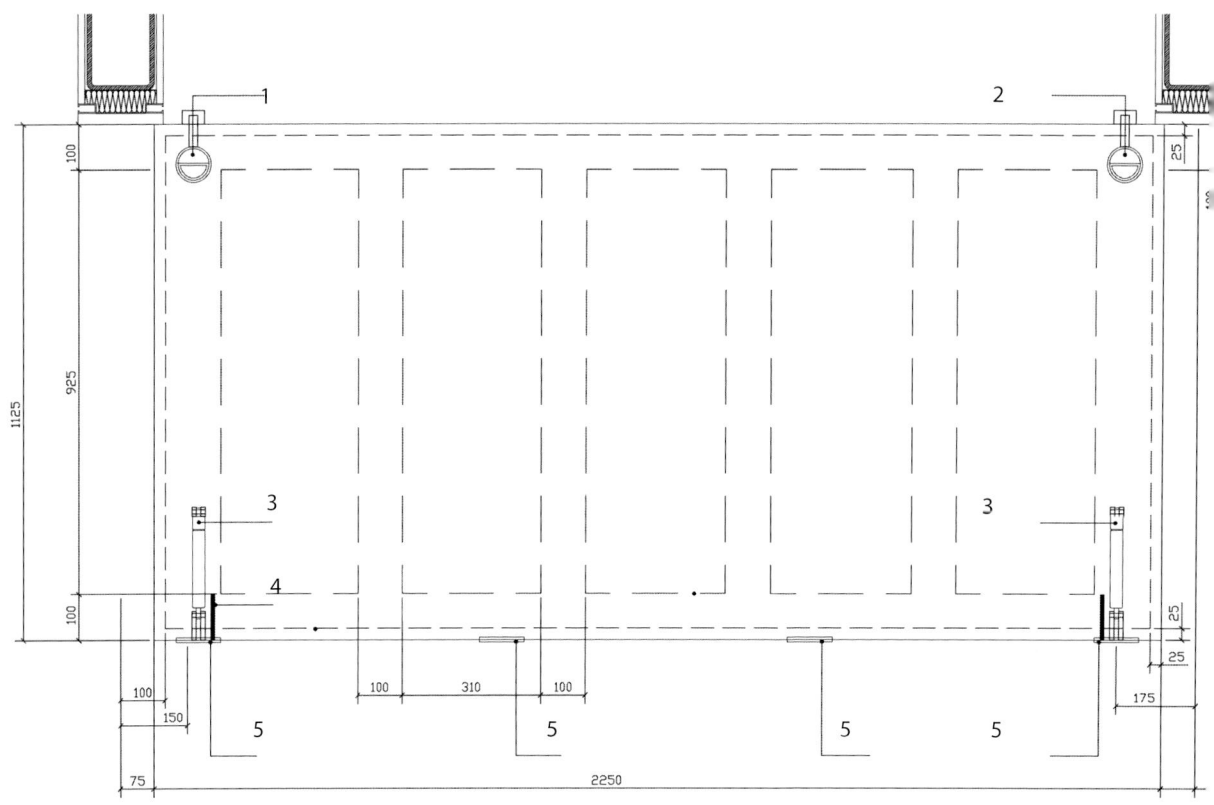

Pneumatically assisted floor panel

1. Location of latch
2. Location of dead-bolt
3. Gas spring
4. Location of hook and eye to hold panel in position
5. Recessed hinge
6. Metal bracket
7. Under panel support

Detail

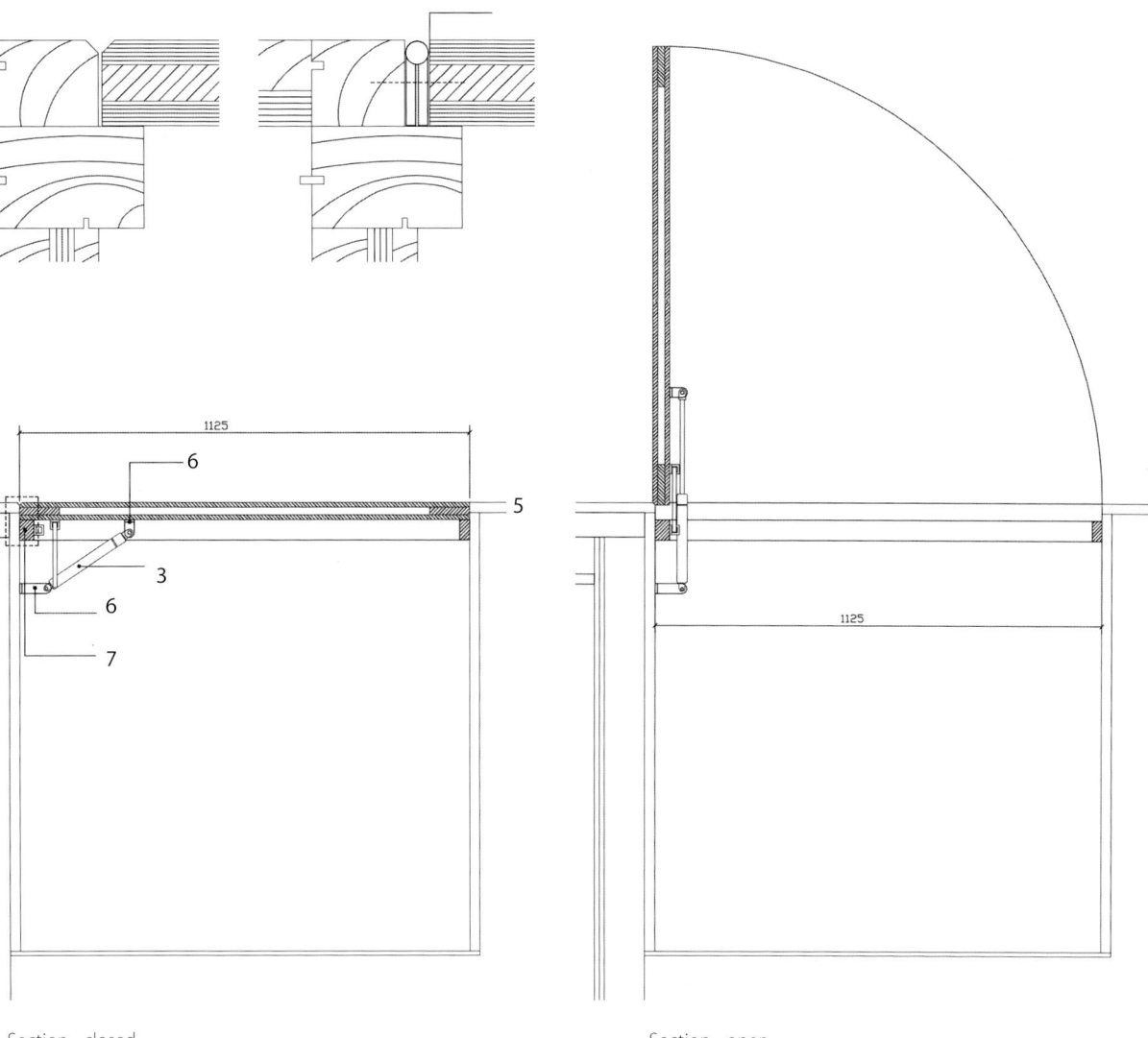

Section - closed

Section - open

José Cruz Ovalle

Study and Home in Vitacura

SANTIAGO DE CHILE, CHILE   *Fotografías: Juan Purcell*

This scheme is located in a neighborhood consisting of single-family dwellings surrounded by large gardens. The area was developed fifty years ago near the river Mapocho that crosses the city of Santiago from east to west. At the present time the neighborhood has been consolidated and occupies a relatively central position in the city.

The 665 m² sites are flanked by a single-family dwelling converted into a store and another dwelling whose garden has an area of approximately one hectare. Inside it stand two separate buildings that create between them a garden-courtyard: the studio next to the street and the dwelling at the rear. The space of the front garden is treated as a public space: it is not fenced off as is habitual in the neighborhood, so the studio has a public rather than a domestic character.

The studio is placed crossways on the site occupying the total width, so its interior space extends on two fronts: toward the street and toward the garden-courtyard of the dwelling. The interior is developed so that there is a complete and flowing perspective of the internal space from any angle - it is an interior in which to linger. This is achieved by retaining the internal void through the articulation of depth without creating a vanishing point. Wooden surfaces fold and unfold to temper the light without producing shade or glare on the work surfaces. Openings and interstices are carefully angled to receive the different types of light entering from different directions according to the time of day and the season.

On the other side, the dwelling, situated at the rear of the site facing the northern sun, opens up toward the garden-courtyard between the two buildings. The volume of the studio, located in front of the house, closes this space and prevents a vanishing point toward the street. It is habitual in Santiago to enter houses from the street, cross them and end up in a living room in front of the garden. This is a way of conceiving space on the basis of the direction. But in this house the order is inverted because one enters the living room from the garden. The architect did not start from isolated directions but tried to redirect the space, managing the depth and controlling the vanishing point. Thus, for example, the arrangement of the diagonal walls in the living room and the thickness between the pillars and the plane of the windows opens a transverse depth that continues through the trees, the grass and the bushes to the facade of the studio.

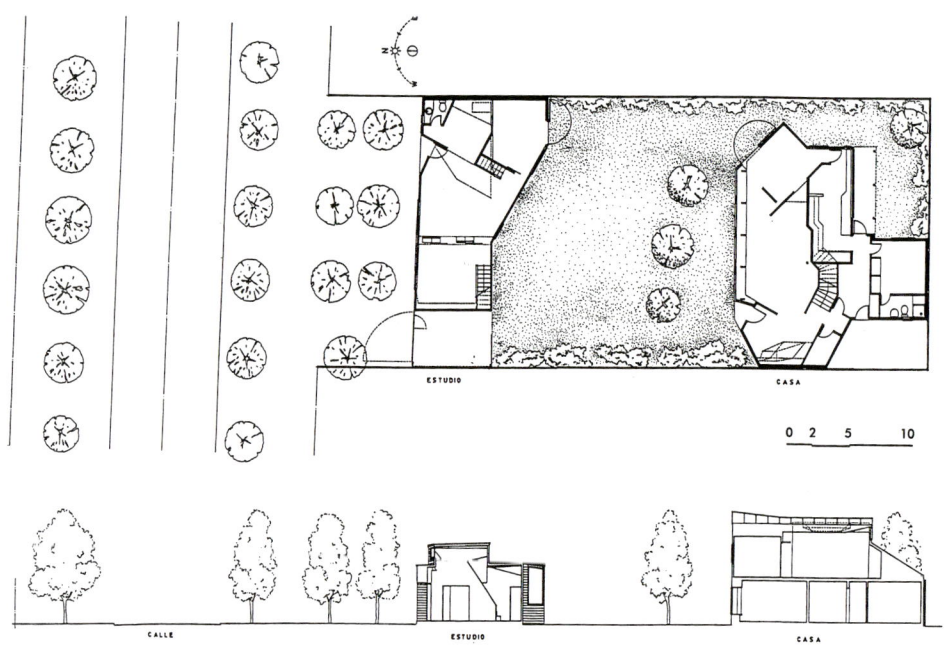

Site plan

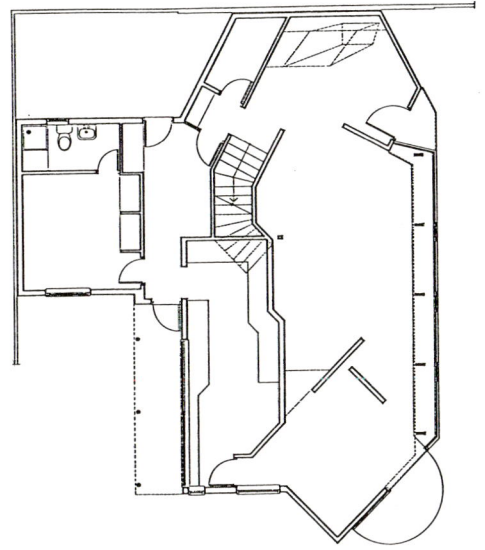

Ground floor plan

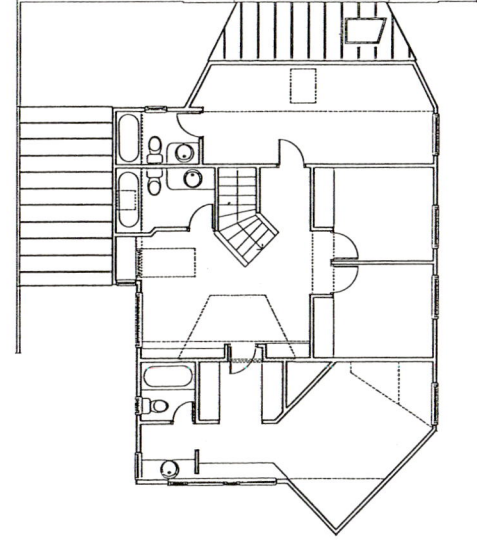

First floor plan

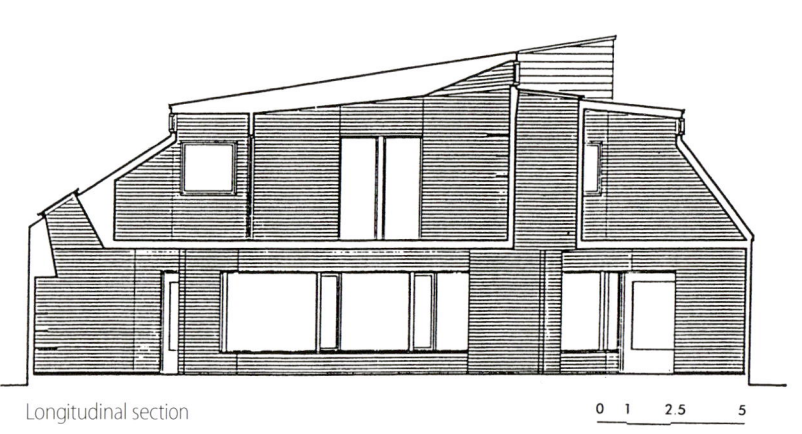

Longitudinal section

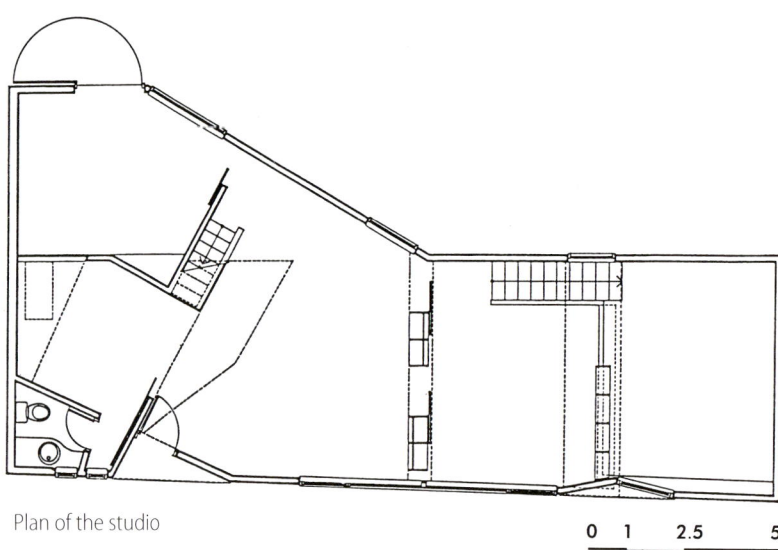

Plan of the studio

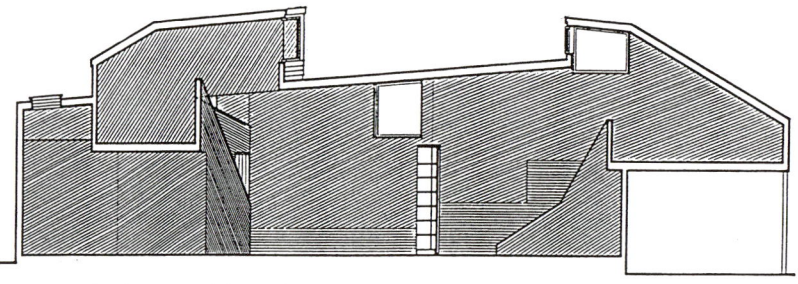

Longitudinal section of the studio

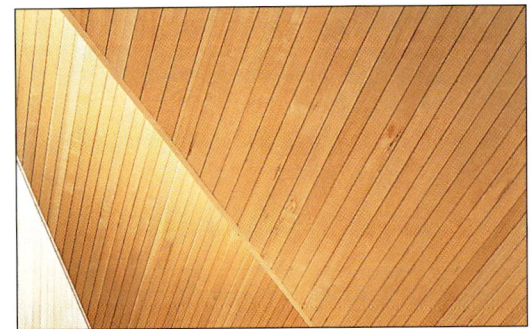

The tempered light is captured without reflections in the interior by means of the articulation of the pleats and folds of the wooden surfaces.

Jean-Pierre Lévêque

Maison Rue Compans

PARIS, FRANCE Photographs: Hervé Abbadie

This building, an old laboratory built in the thirties, was transformed into an inhabitable space after twenty years. It is located in a complex fabric of plots, a kind of residual space in the form of an isosceles triangle between two five-story blocks.

For the rehabilitation of this small dwelling of 80 m^2, the brief was to optimize its habitability and to rediscover in the space a clear legibility and its initial constitution as a building suspended over a covered exterior.

The layout offered the possibility of creating a multi-purpose space defined by the exterior and interior elements. The ground floor was left completely open in order to allow the exterior, consisting of the covered courtyard, to be extended completely into the house. Inside this covered exterior, a differentiated structure containing the kitchen was inserted. This "box" is completely open within the continuous layout of the floor, walls and ceiling, thus giving the dwelling a distinguished appearance.

The exterior of this volume is secured by means of the lower part of the room, and by the pillar that supports it. The house is therefore suspended, with the areas that require greater domestic privacy, such as the bedrooms and the bathroom, at the top.

All the spaces were connected to each other by means of a wooden strip. This begins as the main envelope of the kitchen, becomes the staircase that gives access to the first floor and ends in a wide bookcase before leading to the bedrooms. This "Ariadne's thread", ensures maximum fluidity, multiplying all possible points of view in the area of the dining room and the kitchen in the ascent to the first level, in which all the dimensions of the space that one moves through are apparent.

The basement is accessed by a long flight of stairs that is partially covered by a glass panel. This opening provides natural lighting for the office located in the basement, and accentuates the effect of inclusion of the kitchen volume in the ground floor. the requalification of the environmental context.

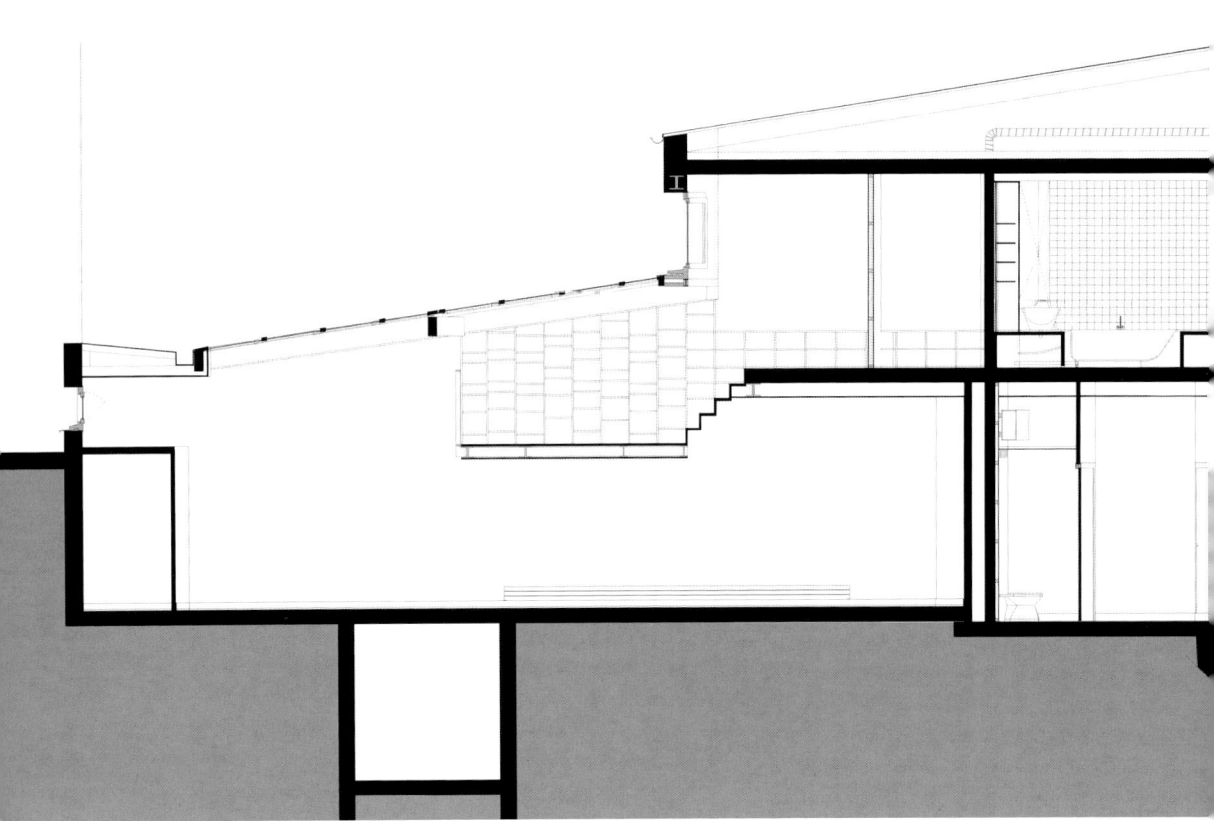
Longitudinal section

257

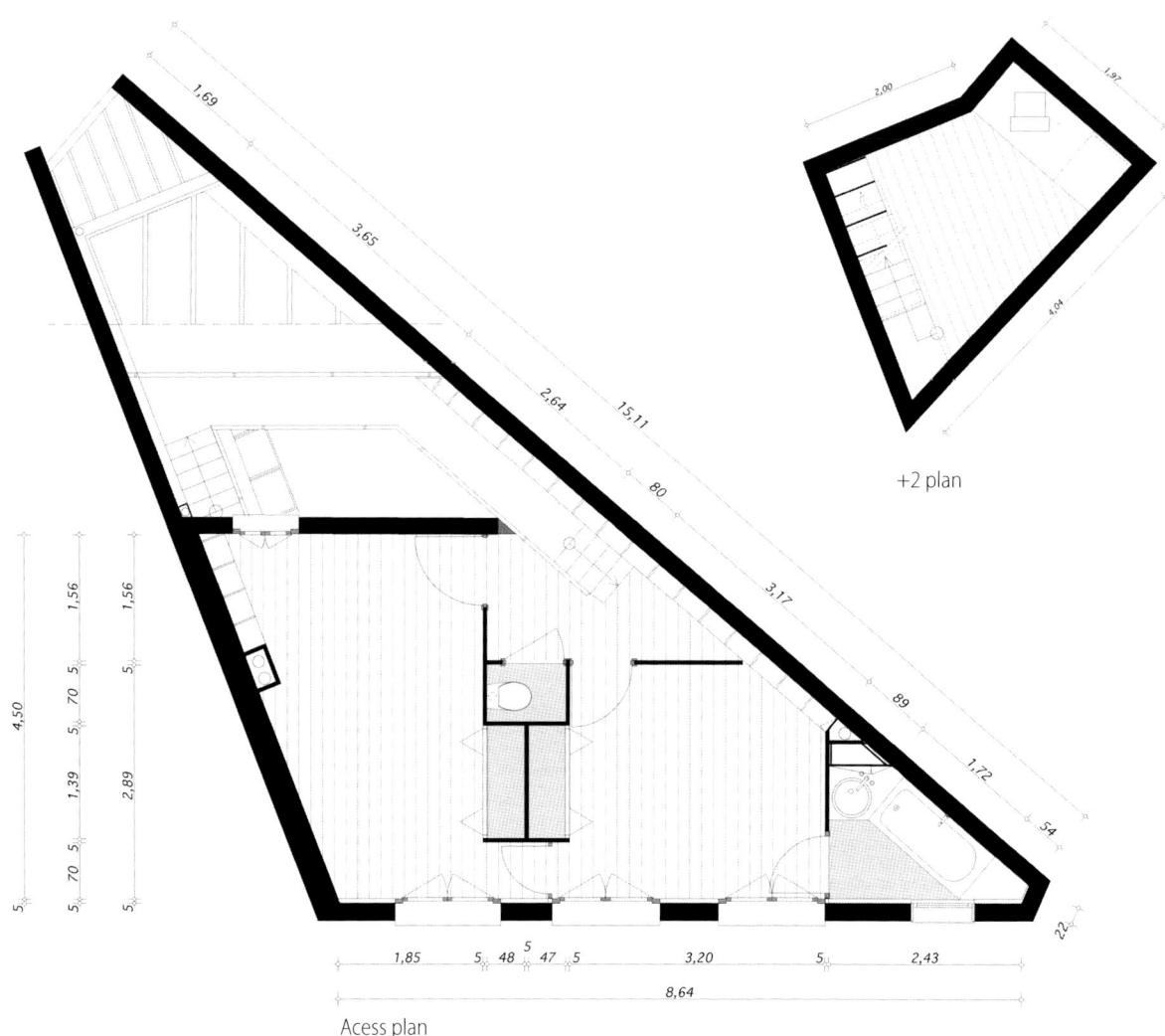

+2 plan

Acess plan

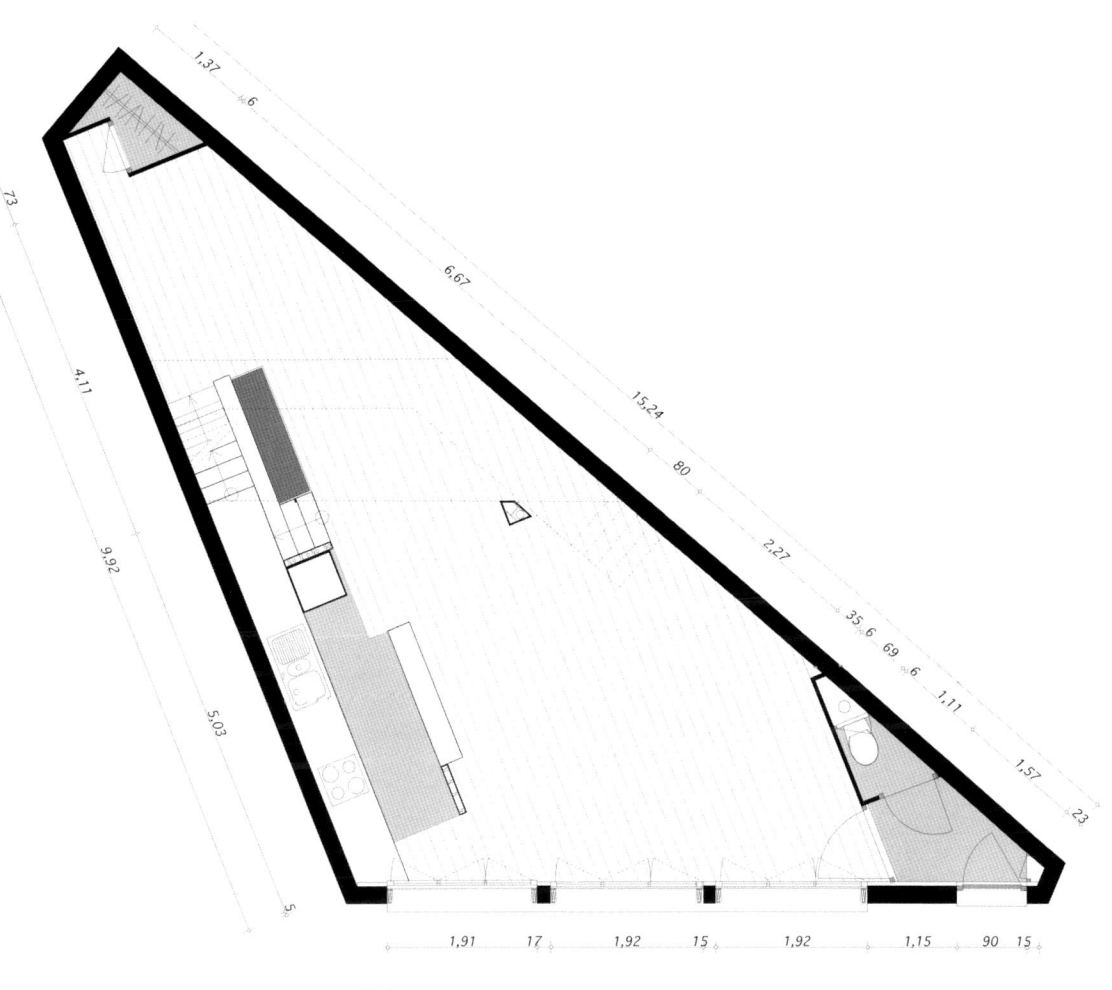

+1 plan

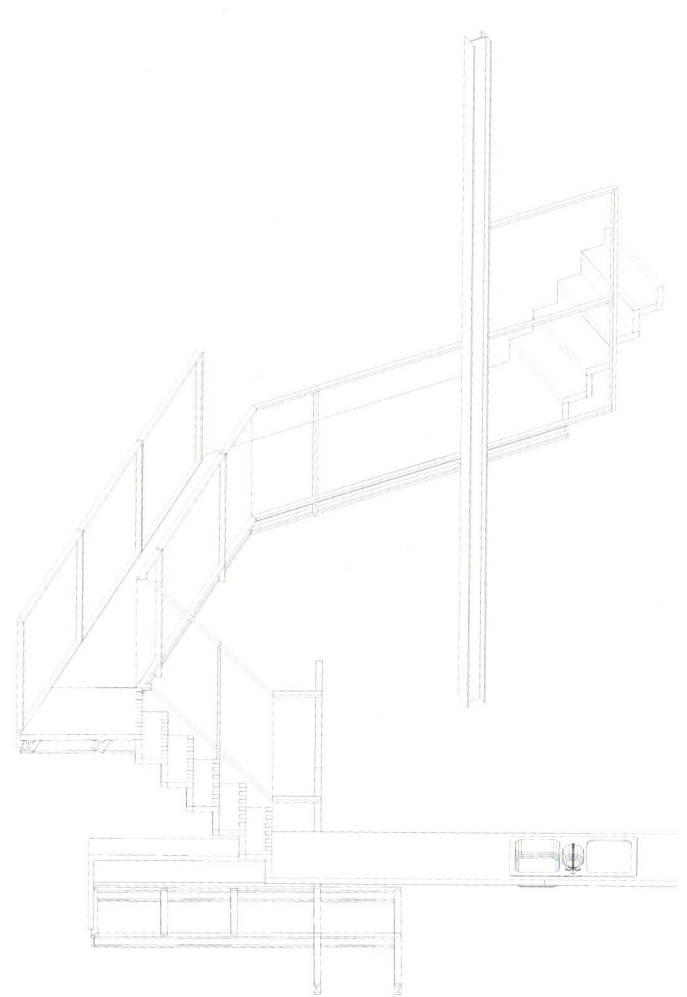
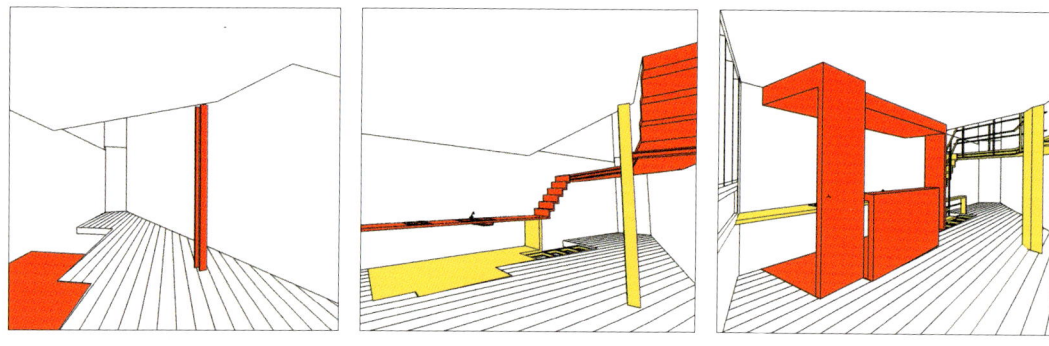

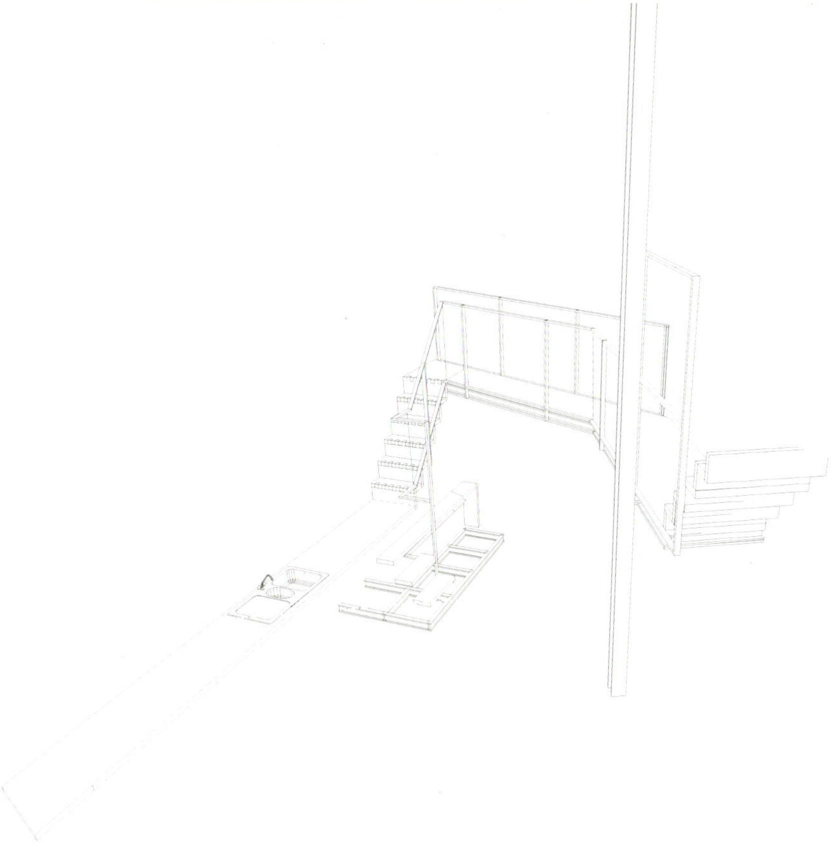

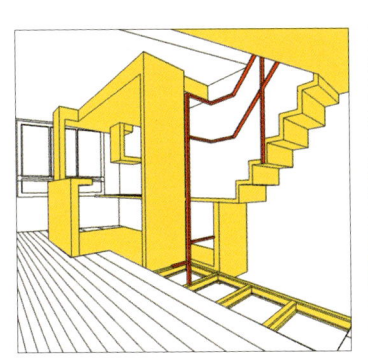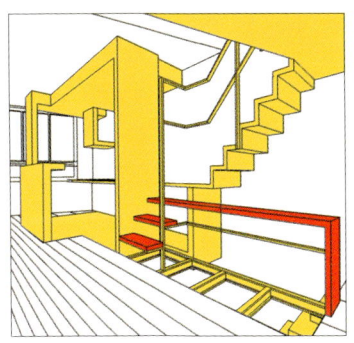

Littow architectes

Paris 6e

París, France　　　　　　　　　　　　　　　　　　　　　　　*Photographs: Pekka Littow*

This apartment occupies the last two floors of a Parisian property built in the 17th century. These last two floors were probably built more recently to house two simpler apartments for the servants. It was later decided to join them to form a single apartment. After a meticulous study of the technical limits of this conversion, the challenge consisted in obtaining a space that was as open as possible. All the existing elements that limited the views or the natural lighting were reduced without sacrificing the hierarchy of the spaces and the structure of the inhabitable areas. It was thus attempted to create subtle and delicate borders that could be adjusted. They are like visual borders that allow for different interpretations. The dining room is isolated from the other rooms by glazed walls, allowing in the natural light from the inner courtyard and from the openings in the guest room. The kitchen forms an integral part of the living room, although it is completely concealed by a set of folding wooden panels, so the appearance of the apartment varies according to the time of day and the needs of its occupants.

The abundance of exposed pillars and wooden props, many of which were completely rotten, called for special treatment and some were eliminated or replaced. The brick walls of the street facade were stripped and according to age-old techniques, showing a craftsman's touch that gives new value to the building.

In the upper room the drop ceilings were removed to reveal magnificent woodwork. The same procedure was applied to the guest room, where a small mezzanine was installed to the right of the volume of the old covered structure. Inside the dwelling, the new spaces that have been created reveal more about the demolition and the subtle unification than about the construction itself. Composing with the existing elements was a priority, but the question was to define what could be changed, what had to be conserved and how to deal with it. The first rule was that the original structures should be the dominant ones, the new elements only playing a secondary role.

The furniture was designed by the architect and made specially for these spaces with the aim of creating a relaxing atmosphere

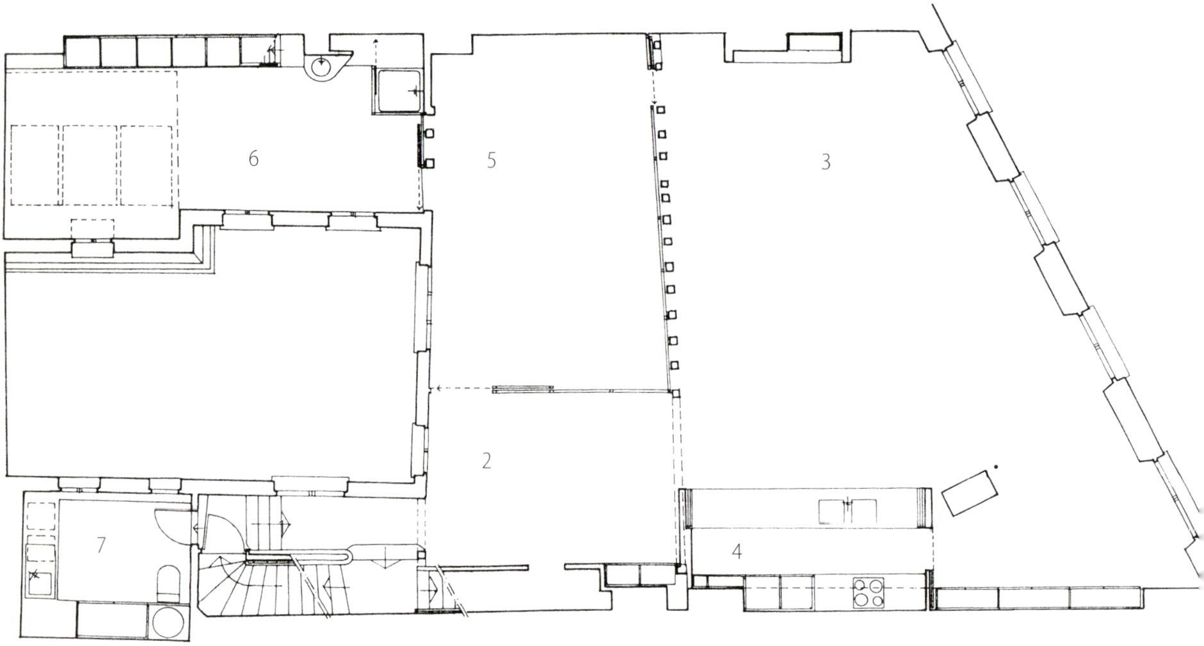

266

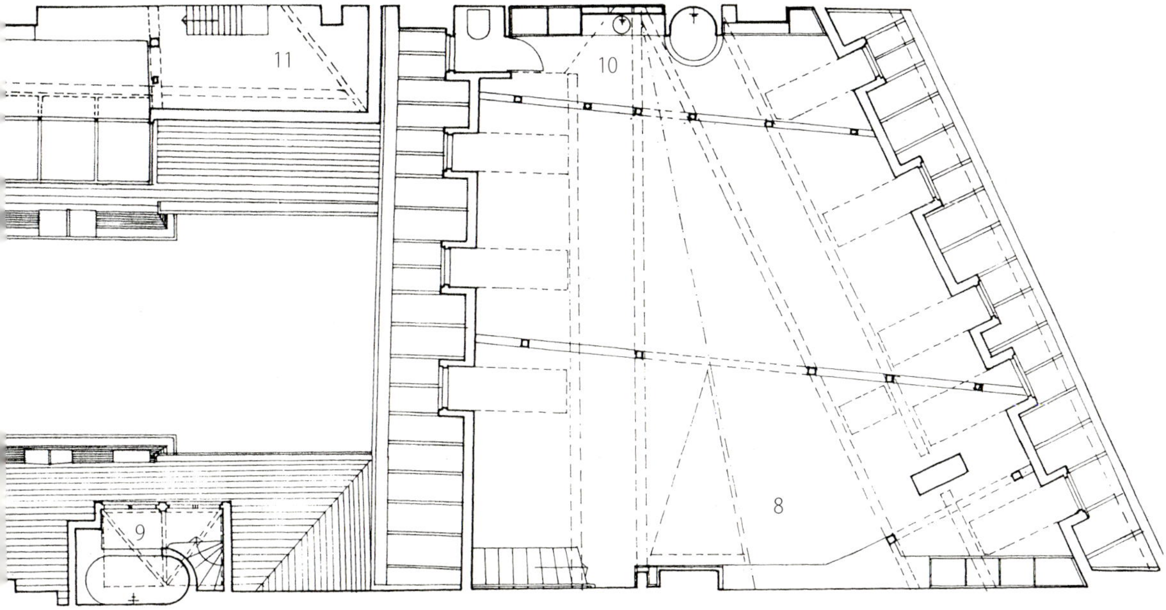

267

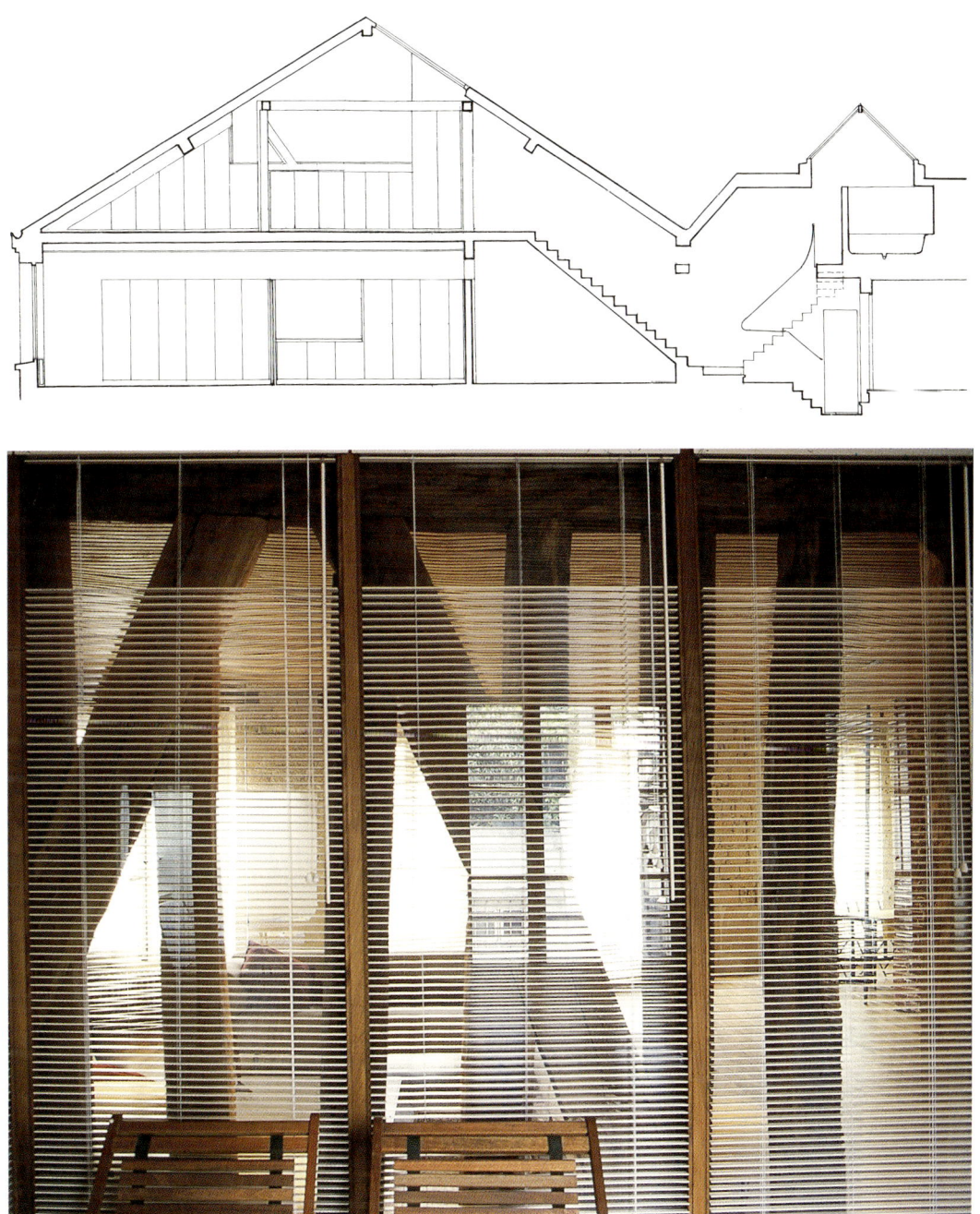

Arnaud Goujon Architecte DPLG

Transformed penthouse

PARIS, FRANCE *Photographs: Joel Cariou*

In the heart of Paris, the architect Arnaud Goujon transformed an old greenhouse located at the top of a block of flats into a small and comfortable refuge with a terrace and unique views. Conceived as an extension of the loft apartment, this volume would soon become the favorite room of this home. It is a scheme in which the initial volumetrics was respected and a new wooden frame was superimposed on the steel structure. On the exterior, the shingle boards are made of red Canadian cedar, while the interior walls are lined with moabi panels.

The main task for the architect in this rehabilitation –apart from the technical problems– consisted of designing and organizing the different spaces of the apartment, and resolving the problems of execution and assembly of the different materials. The absence of exposed fittings on the wall panels of the interior helps to enlarge and unify the volume of the main room, which opens on both sides onto a terrace of 50 m2 covered with a jatoba wood deck and offering spectacular views of the urban landscape.

The interior of this unusual dwelling is composed only of a living room with an open integrated kitchen, in which a chimney is framed between two shelves, and a small bedroom with its bathroom. This room enjoys the benefit of two sources of natural light that illuminate this more private area: a small window in the back wall and a skylight located over the bed. The floor of the interior is made of chestnut parquet covered with white polyurethane paint that reduces the color saturation and brings freshness to the dwelling.

The wood, chosen for its plastic and structural qualities, is used as a double skin: soft and beautiful in the interior and rough and sturdy on the exterior. Thus, although this organic material is set against the urban nature of an environment in which steel is the main component, its form fits well into the geometric pattern of the building.

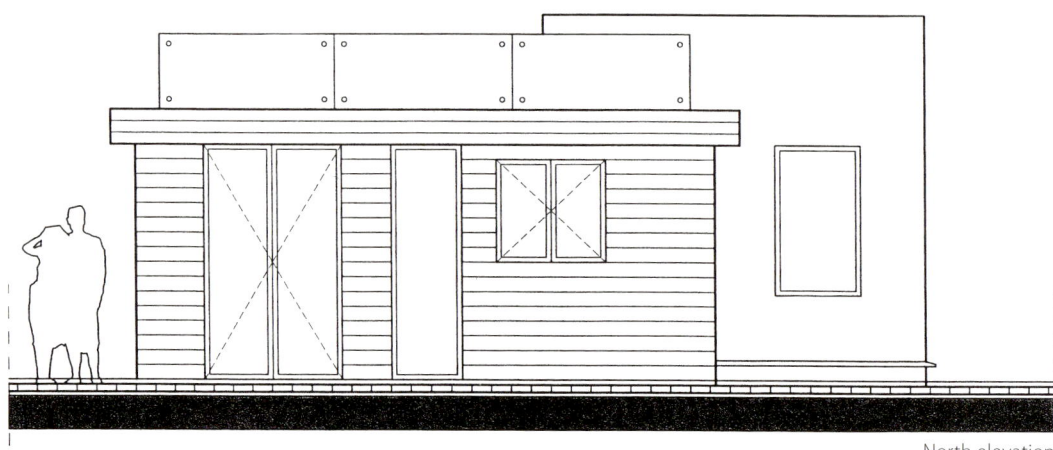

North elevation

The terrace running round this apartment is one of its fundamental elements. The panoramic views of Paris are an additional feature that enhances the architectural work.

East elevation

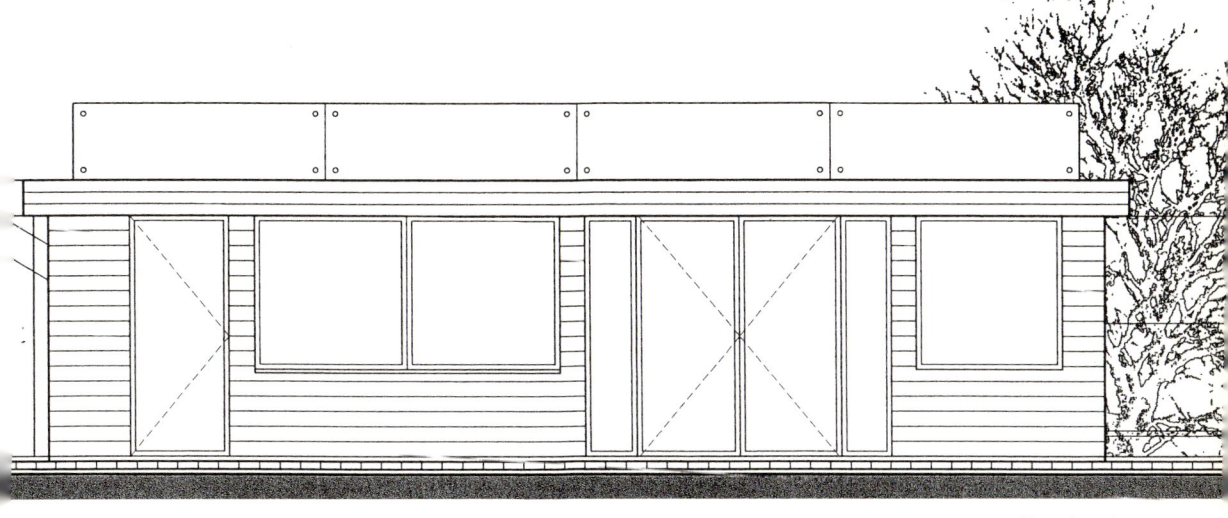

The wood, chosen for its plastic and structural qualities, is used as a double skin: soft and beautiful in the interior and rough and sturdy on the exterior.

The interior of this unusual dwelling is composed only of a living room with an open integrated kitchen, in which a chimney is framed between two shelves, and a small bedroom with its bathroom. This room enjoys the benefit of two sources of natural light that illuminate this more private area: a small window in the back wall and a skylight located over the bed.

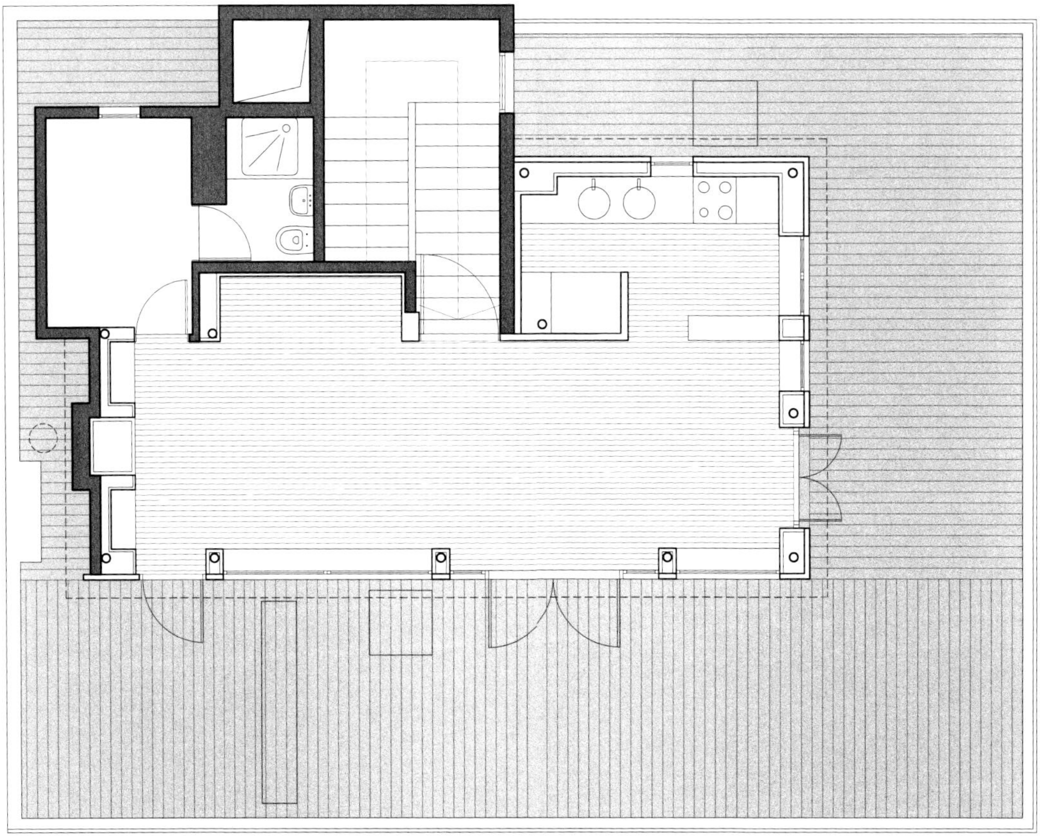

Floor plan

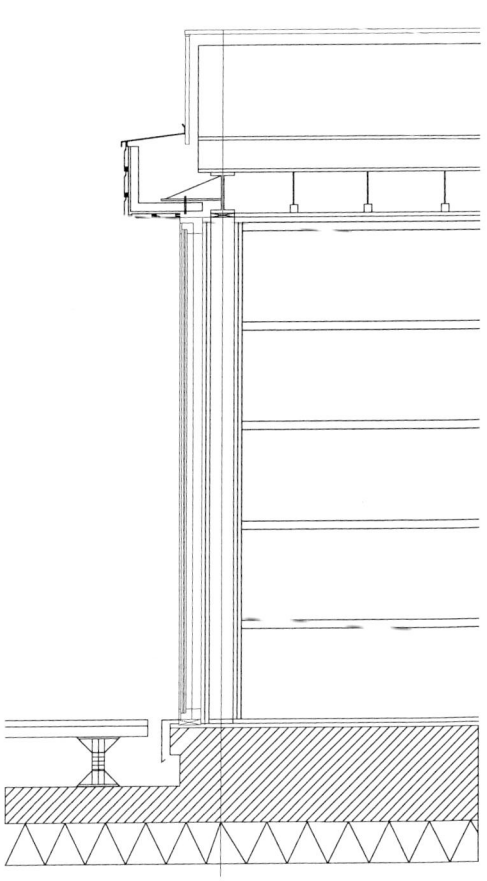

Vertical section on window

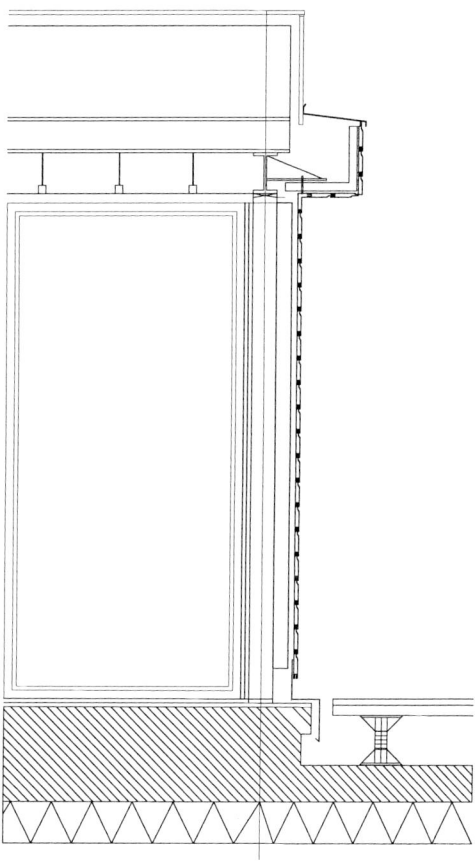

Vertical section on wood wall

Jarmund / Vigsnaes Architects

Red House

OSLO, NORWAY *Photographs: Nils Petter Dale*

Oslo is a vast city that spreads up the sides of its bowl from its old center into the hills and forests of a gentle, though still wild-looking, landscape. The Red House was built in one of the lovely wooded western suburbs, in this case dominated by postwar detached houses, carefully sited among the trees to maximize contact with a nature that appears untouched but is in fact tamed by electricity, mains drainage and modern roads.

The site for the house is the steep east bank of a heavily wooded river valley. The rectangular floor plan is at right angles to the slope, with the entrance at the east end of the upper level. The building is placed perpendicular to the stream to heighten the dynamic potential of the setting and to avoid obstructing the view from the house uphill, in the sprawling garden of which the new building has been built.

The house is organized on two floors. Living spaces and the master bedroom are on the entrance level, oriented towards the south and the view. This level culminates in a covered terrace among the trees to the west, where the river below can be glimpsed through the trees. But the most dramatic views are to the south, across the stream and over a forest.

The lower floor houses the children's bedrooms, facing the river valley to the north beneath the trees.

This double orientation is the basis for the architectonic dynamic of the project, and all aspects of the design are focused on enhancing this theme. Construction is conventional, with a timber frame over a basement floor that has been partly cut into the hillside. The postwar wooden single family houses that characterize the neighborhood have inspired both the development of the spatial concept and the detailing. The use of color reflects the temperament of the client.

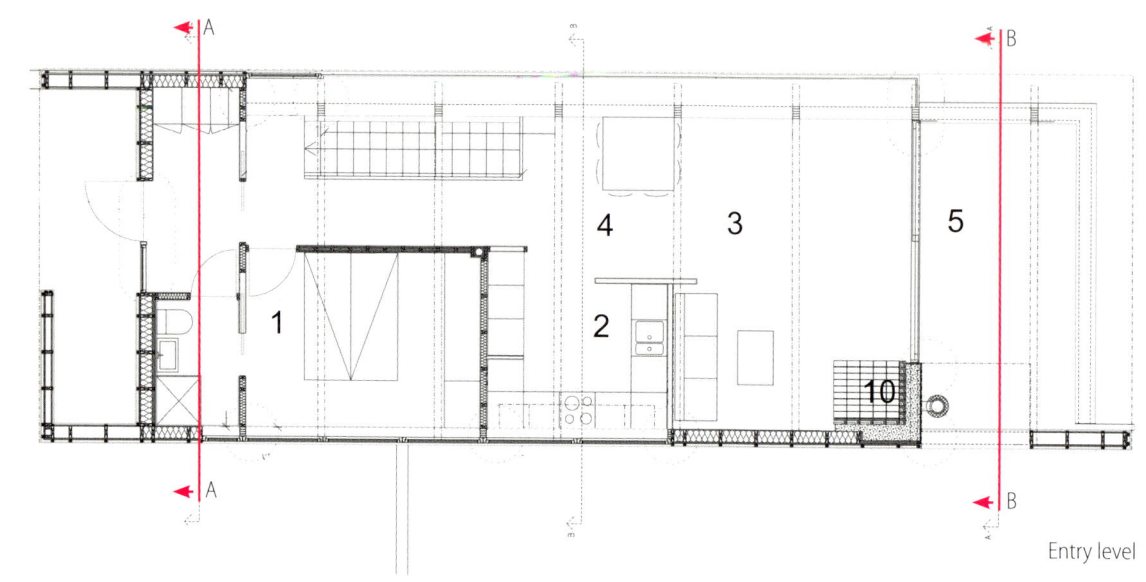

Entry level

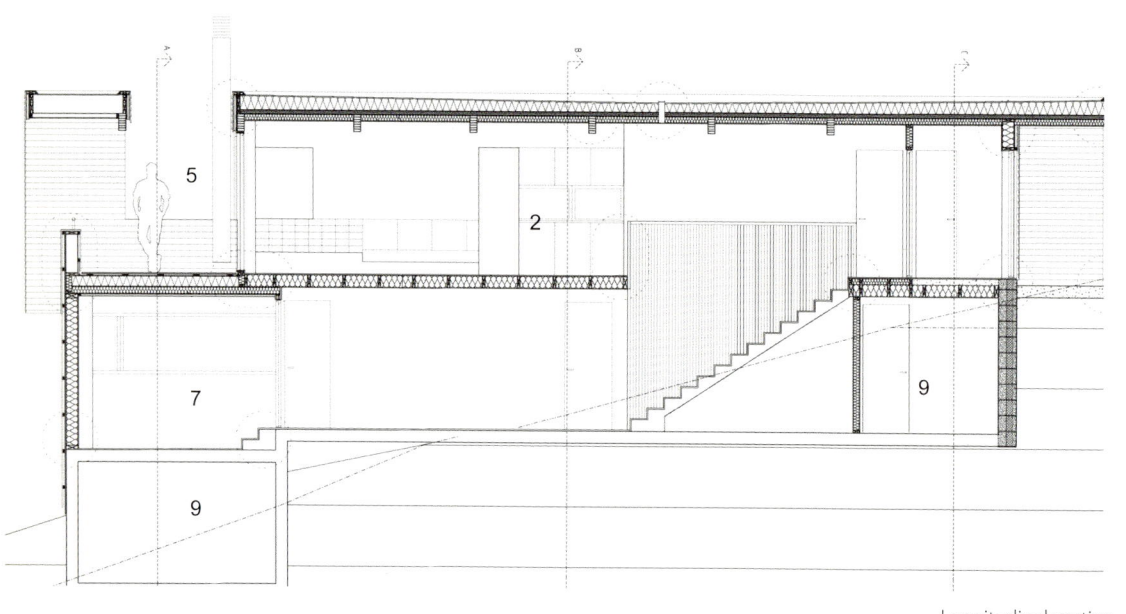

Longitudinal section

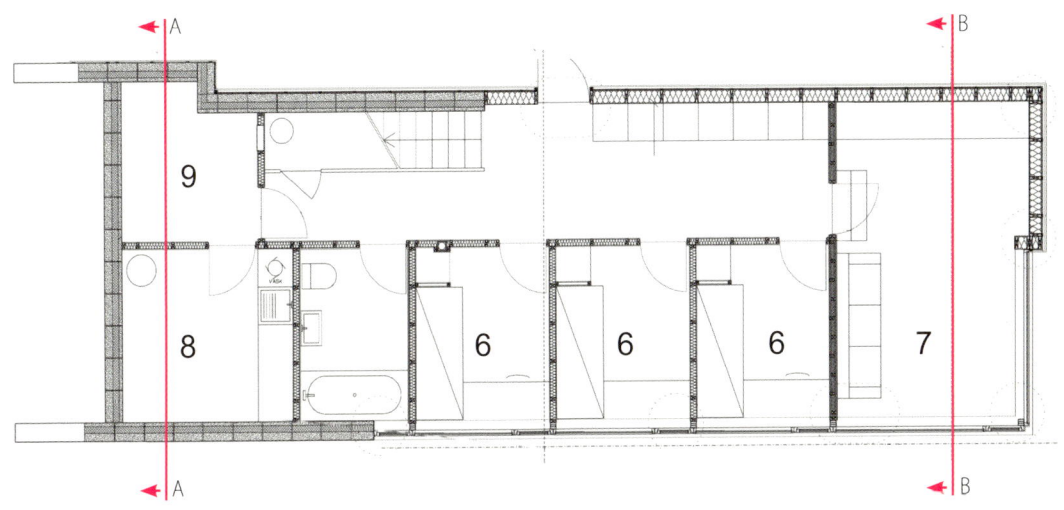

Lower level

1. Master bedroom
2. Kitchen
3. Living
4. Dining
5. Terrace
6. Bedroom
7. Playroom
8. Laundry
9. Storage
10. Fireplace

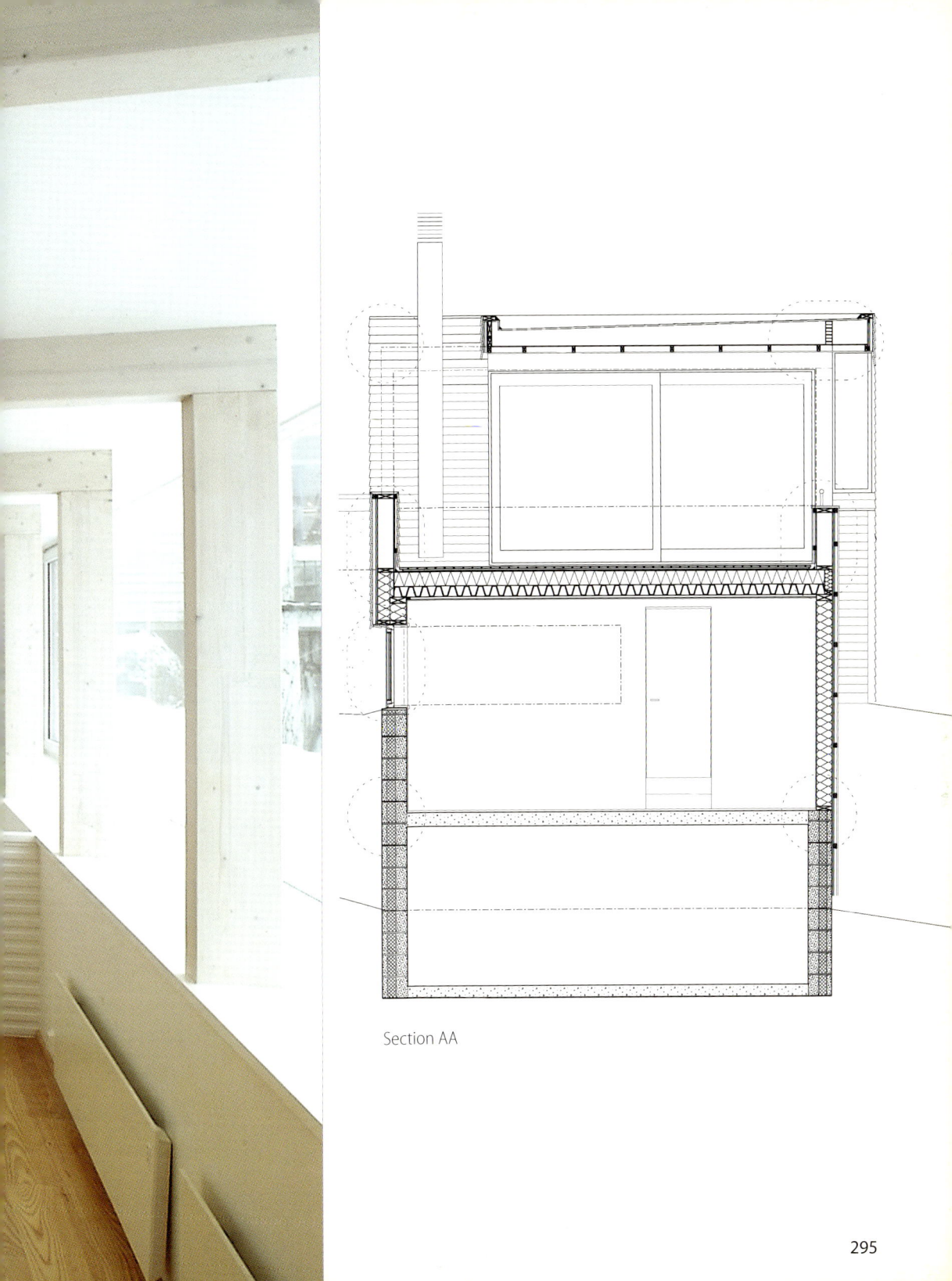
Section AA

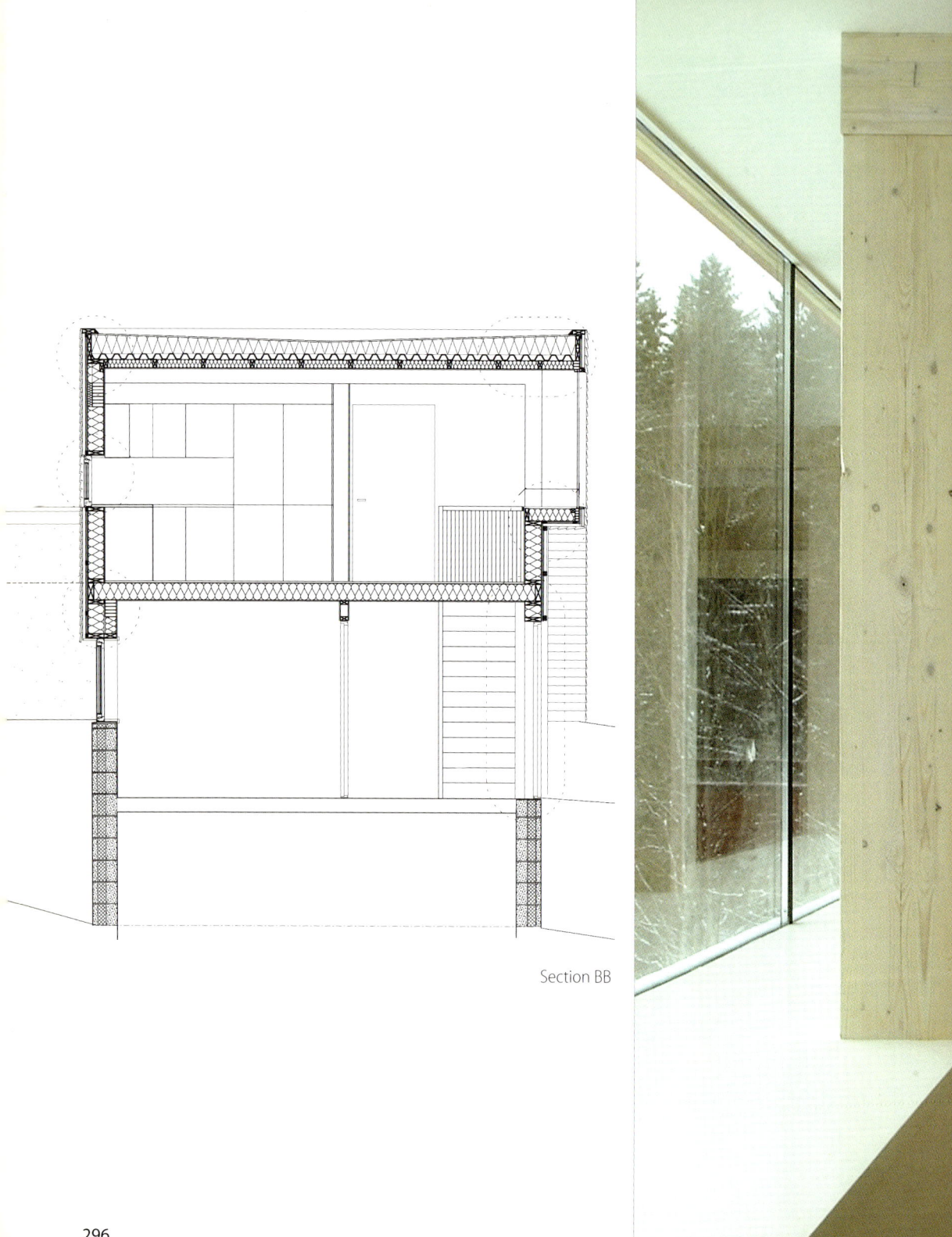

Section BB